Cram101 Textbook Outlines to accompany:

Intermediate Microeconomics

Varian, 6th Edition

An Academic Internet Publishers (AIPI) publication (c) 2007.

You have a discounted membership at www.Cram101.com with this book.

Get all of the practice tests for the chapters of this textbook, and access in-depth reference material for writing essays and papers. Here is an example from a Cram101 Biology text:

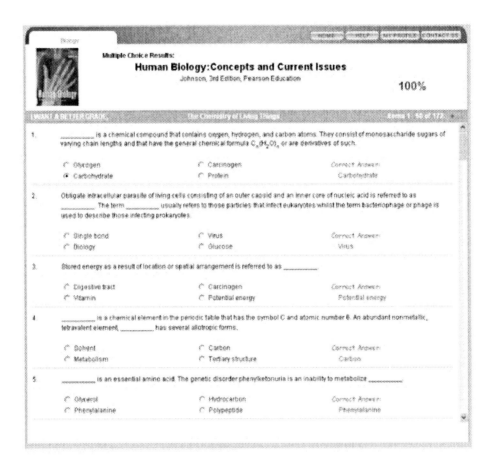

When you need problem solving help with math, stats, and other disciplines, www.Cram101.com will walk through the formulas and solutions step by step.

With Cram101.com online, you also have access to extensive reference material.

You will nail those essays and papers. Here is an example from a Cram101 Biology text:

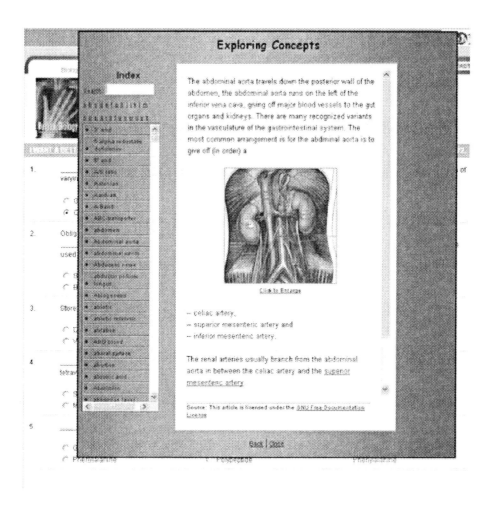

Learning System

Cram101 Textbook Outlines is a learning system. The notes in this book are the highlights of your textbook, you will never have to highlight a book again.

How to use this book. Take this book to class, it is your notebook for the lecture. The notes and highlights on the left hand side of the pages follow the outline and order of the textbook. All you have to do is follow along while your intructor presents the lecture. Circle the items emphasized in class and add other important information on the right side. With Cram101 Textbook Outlines you'll spend less time writing and more time listening. Learning becomes more efficient.

Cram101.com Online

Increase your studying efficiency by using Cram101.com's practice tests and online reference material. It is the perfect complement to Cram101 Textbook Outlines. Use self-teaching matching tests or simulate in-class testing with comprehensive multiple choice tests, or simply use Cram's true and false tests for quick review. Cram101.com even allows you to enter your in-class notes for an integrated studying format combining the textbook notes with your class notes.

Visit **www.Cram101.com**, click Sign Up at the top of the screen, and enter **DK73DW2303** in the promo code box on the registration screen. Access to www.Cram101.com is normally $9.95, but because you have purchased this book, your access fee is only $4.95. Sign up and stop highlighting textbooks forever.

Intermediate Microeconomics
Varian, 6th

CONTENTS

Intermediate Microeconomics
Varian, 6th

CONTENTS (continued)

Economics	The social science dealing with the use of scarce resources to obtain the maximum satisfaction of society's virtually unlimited economic wants is an economics.
Market	A market is, as defined in economics, a social arrangement that allows buyers and sellers to discover information and carry out a voluntary exchange of goods or services.
Exogenous variable	Exogenous variable refers to a variable that is taken as given by an economic model. It therefore is subject to direct manipulation by the modeler. In most models, policy variables such as tariffs and par values of pegged exchange rates are exogenous.
Variable	A variable is something measured by a number; it is used to analyze what happens to other things when the size of that number changes.
Endogenous variable	Endogenous variable refers to an economic variable that is determined within a model. It is therefore not subject to direct manipulation by the modeler, since that would override the model.
Demand curve	Demand curve refers to the graph of quantity demanded as a function of price, normally downward sloping, straight or curved, and drawn with quantity on the horizontal axis and price on the vertical axis.
Consumption	In Keynesian economics consumption refers to personal consumption expenditure, i.e., the purchase of currently produced goods and services out of income, out of savings (net worth), or from borrowed funds. It refers to that part of disposable income that does not go to saving.
Supply	Supply is the aggregate amount of any material good that can be called into being at a certain price point; it comprises one half of the equation of supply and demand. In classical economic theory, a curve representing supply is one of the factors that produce price.
Rental price	The payment per unit time for the services of a unit of a factor of production, such as land or capital is called rental price.
Equilibrium price	Equilibrium price refers to the price in a competitive market at which the quantity demanded and the quantity supplied are equal, there is neither a shortage nor a surplus, and there is no tendency for price to rise or fall.
Economic agents	Economic agents refers to individuals who engage in production, exchange, specialization, and consumption.
Agent	A person who makes economic decisions for another economic actor. A hired manager operates as an agent for a firm's owner.
Willingness to pay	Willingness to pay refers to the largest amount of money that an individual or group could pay, along with a change in policy, without being made worse off.
Market price	Market price is an economic concept with commonplace familiarity; it is the price that a good or service is offered at, or will fetch, in the marketplace; it is of interest mainly in the study of microeconomics.
Quantity demanded	The amount of a good or service that buyers desire to purchase at a particular price during some period is a quantity demanded.
Slope	The slope of a line in the plane containing the x and y axes is generally represented by the letter m, and is defined as the change in the y coordinate divided by the corresponding change in the x coordinate, between two distinct points on the line.
Supply curve	Supply curve refers to the graph of quantity supplied as a function of price, normally upward sloping, straight or curved, and drawn with quantity on the horizontal axis and price on the vertical axis.
Interest	In finance and economics, interest is the price paid by a borrower for the use of a lender's money. In other words, interest is the amount of paid to "rent" money for a period of time.
Supply and	The partial equilibrium supply and demand economic model originally developed by Alfred Marshall

demand	attempts to describe, explain, and predict changes in the price and quantity of goods sold in competitive markets.
Comparative static	The comparison of two equilibria from a static model, usually differing by the effects of a single small change in an exogenous variable is a comparative static.
Economic model	Economic model refers to a simplified picture of economic reality; an abstract generalization.
Comparative statics	Comparative statics is the comparison of two different equilibrium states, before and after a change in one of the variables. Being a study of statics it compares two different unchanging points, once they have changed. It does not study the motion towards equilibrium, nor the process of the change itself.
Allocate	Allocate refers to the assignment of income for various tax purposes. A multistate corporation's nonbusiness income usually is distributed to the state where the nonbusiness assets are located; it is not apportioned with the rest of the entity's income.
Monopoly	A monopoly is defined as a persistent market situation where there is only one provider of a kind of product or service.
Auction	A preexisting business model that operates successfully on the Internet by announcing an item for sale and permitting multiple purchasers to bid on them under specified rules and condition is an auction.
Competitive market	A market in which no buyer or seller has market power is called a competitive market.
Profit	Profit refers to the return to the resource entrepreneurial ability; total revenue minus total cost.
Revenue	Revenue is a U.S. business term for the amount of money that a company receives from its activities, mostly from sales of products and/or services to customers.
Tenant	The party to whom the leasehold is transferred is a tenant. A leasehold estate is an ownership interest in land in which a lessee or a tenant holds real property by some form of title from a lessor or landlord.
Scope	Scope of a project is the sum total of all projects products and their requirements or features.
Market system	All the product and resource markets of a market economy and the relationships among them are called a market system.
Pareto efficiency	A condition in which no change is possible that will make some members of society better off without making some other members of society worse off is referred to as pareto efficiency. It is a central concept in economics with broad applications in game theory, engineering and the social sciences.
Economic efficiency	Economic efficiency refers to the use of the minimum necessary resources to obtain the socially optimal amounts of goods and services; entails both productive efficiency and allocative efficiency.
Strike	The withholding of labor services by an organized group of workers is referred to as a strike.
Gain	In finance, gain is a profit or an increase in value of an investment such as a stock or bond. Gain is calculated by fair market value or the proceeds from the sale of the investment minus the sum of the purchase price and all costs associated with it.
Swap	In finance a swap is a derivative, where two counterparties exchange one stream of cash flows against another stream. These streams are called the legs of the swap. The cash flows are calculated over a notional principal amount. Swaps are often used to hedge certain risks, for instance interest rate risk. Another use is speculation.
Incentive	An incentive is any factor (financial or non-financial) that provides a motive for a particular course of action, or counts as a reason for preferring one choice to the alternatives.
Pareto efficient	Pareto efficient allocation refers to an allocation of resources in which no one individual can be made better off without making someone else worse off.

allocation	
Efficient allocation	An allocation that it is impossible unambiguously to improve upon, in the sense of producing more of one good without producing less of another is an efficient allocation.
Distribution	Distribution in economics, the manner in which total output and income is distributed among individuals or factors.
Long run	In economic models, the long run time frame assumes no fixed factors of production. Firms can enter or leave the marketplace, and the cost (and availability) of land, labor, raw materials, and capital goods can be assumed to vary.
Gains from trade	The net increase in output that countries experience as a result of lowering import tariffs and otherwise liberalizing trade is referred to as gains from trade.
Assignment	A transfer of property or some right or interest is referred to as assignment.
Argument	The discussion by counsel for the respective parties of their contentions on the law and the facts of the case being tried in order to aid the jury in arriving at a correct and just conclusion is called argument.
Short run	Short run refers to a period of time that permits an increase or decrease in current production volume with existing capacity, but one that is too short to permit enlargement of that capacity itself (eg, the building of new plants, training of additional workers, etc.).
Economic analysis	The process of deriving economic principles from relevant economic facts are called economic analysis. It is the comparison, with money as the index, of those costs and benefits to the wider economy that can be reasonably quantified, including all social costs and benefits of a project.

Budget constraint	Budget constraint refers to the maximum quantity of goods that could be purchased for a given level of income and a given set of prices.
Budget	Budget refers to an account, usually for a year, of the planned expenditures and the expected receipts of an entity. For a government, the receipts are tax revenues.
Consumption	In Keynesian economics consumption refers to personal consumption expenditure, i.e., the purchase of currently produced goods and services out of income, out of savings (net worth), or from borrowed funds. It refers to that part of disposable income that does not go to saving.
Budget line	Given an allocation of two goods, the budget line through that allocation is the set of all other allocations of the two goods that someone in a market could arrive at by selling one of the goods for the other.
Budget set	A budget set includes all possible consumption bundles that someone can afford given the prices of goods and the person's income level. The budget set is bounded above by the budget line.
Property	Assets defined in the broadest legal sense. Property includes the unrealized receivables of a cash basis taxpayer, but not services rendered.
Points	Loan origination fees that may be deductible as interest by a buyer of property. A seller of property who pays points reduces the selling price by the amount of the points paid for the buyer.
Slope	The slope of a line in the plane containing the x and y axes is generally represented by the letter m, and is defined as the change in the y coordinate divided by the corresponding change in the x coordinate, between two distinct points on the line.
Opportunity cost	The cost of something in terms of opportunity foregone. The opportunity cost to a country of producing a unit more of a good, such as for export or to replace an import, is the quantity of some other good that could have been produced instead.
Economic cost	Economic cost refers to payments made or incomes forgone to obtain and retain the services of a resource.
Yield	The interest rate that equates a future value or an annuity to a given present value is a yield.
Numeraire	The unit in which prices are measured. This may be a currency, but in real models, such as most trade models, the numeraire is usually one of the goods, whose price is then set at one.
Variable	A variable is something measured by a number; it is used to analyze what happens to other things when the size of that number changes.
Economic policy	Economic policy refers to the actions that governments take in the economic field. It covers the systems for setting interest rates and government deficit as well as the labor market, national ownership, and many other areas of government.
Rationing	Rationing is the controlled distribution of resources and scarce goods or services: it restricts how much people are allowed to buy or consume.
Subsidy	Subsidy refers to government financial assistance to a domestic producer.
Policy	Similar to a script in that a policy can be a less than completely rational decision-making method. Involves the use of a pre-existing set of decision steps for any problem that presents itself.
Total cost	The sum of fixed cost and variable cost is referred to as total cost.
Sales tax	A sales tax is a tax on consumption. It is normally a certain percentage that is added onto

the price of a good or service that is purchased.

Household
An economic unit that provides the economy with resources and uses the income received to purchase goods and services that satisfy economic wants is called household.

Allotment
In terms of finance, an allotment is a method of distributing securities to investors when an issue has been oversubscribed. At the end of the subscription period, the demand for a new issue can exceed the number of shares or bonds being issued.

Coupon
In finance, a coupon is "attached" to a bond, either physically (as with old bonds) or electronically. Each coupon represents a predetermined payment promized to the bond-holder in return for his or her loan of money to the bond-issuer. .

Enterprise
Enterprise refers to another name for a business organization. Other similar terms are business firm, sometimes simply business, sometimes simply firm, as well as company, and entity.

Inflation
An increase in the overall price level of an economy, usually as measured by the CPI or by the implicit price deflator is called inflation.

Go to **Cram101.com** for the Practice Tests for this Chapter.

Consumption	In Keynesian economics consumption refers to personal consumption expenditure, i.e., the purchase of currently produced goods and services out of income, out of savings (net worth), or from borrowed funds. It refers to that part of disposable income that does not go to saving.
Preference	The act of a debtor in paying or securing one or more of his creditors in a manner more favorable to them than to other creditors or to the exclusion of such other creditors is a preference. In the absence of statute, a preference is perfectly good, but to be legal it must be bona fide, and not a mere subterfuge of the debtor to secure a future benefit to himself or to prevent the application of his property to his debts.
Consumer theory	Consumer theory is a theory of economics. It relates preferences, indifference curves and budget constraints to consumer demand curves. The mathematical models that make up consumer theory can be used in a constrained optimization problem to estimate the optimal goods bundle for an individual buyer.
Economic analysis	The process of deriving economic principles from relevant economic facts are called economic analysis. It is the comparison, with money as the index, of those costs and benefits to the wider economy that can be reasonably quantified, including all social costs and benefits of a project.
Property	Assets defined in the broadest legal sense. Property includes the unrealized receivables of a cash basis taxpayer, but not services rendered.
Indifference curve	Indifference curve refers to a means of representing the preferences and well being of consumers. Formally, it is a curve representing the combinations of arguments in a utility function that yield a given level of utility.
Perfect substitute	A good that is regarded by its demanders as identical to another good, so that the elasticity of substitution between them is infinite is referred to as perfect substitute.
Slope	The slope of a line in the plane containing the x and y axes is generally represented by the letter m, and is defined as the change in the y coordinate divided by the corresponding change in the x coordinate, between two distinct points on the line.
Complement	A good that is used in conjunction with another good is a complement. For example, cameras and film would complement eachother.
Perfect complements	Two goods with right-angle indifference curves are perfect complements. Complements are products consumed simultaneously.
Commodity	Could refer to any good, but in trade a commodity is usually a raw material or primary product that enters into international trade, such as metals or basic agricultural products.
Points	Loan origination fees that may be deductible as interest by a buyer of property. A seller of property who pays points reduces the selling price by the amount of the points paid for the buyer.
Economics	The social science dealing with the use of scarce resources to obtain the maximum satisfaction of society's virtually unlimited economic wants is an economics.
Marginal rate of substitution	In economics, the marginal rate of substitution is the rate at which consumers are willing to give up units of one good in exchange for more units of another good.
Exchange	The trade of things of value between buyer and seller so that each is better off after the trade is called the exchange.
Exchange rate	Exchange rate refers to the price at which one country's currency trades for another, typically on the exchange market.
Margin	A deposit by a buyer in stocks with a seller or a stockbroker, as security to cover

Go to **Cram101.com** for the Practice Tests for this Chapter.

fluctuations in the market in reference to stocks that the buyer has purchased but for which he has not paid is a margin. Commodities are also traded on margin.

Rate of exchange	Rate of exchange refers to the price paid in one's own money to acquire 1 unit of a foreign currency; the rate at which the money of one nation is exchanged for the money of another nation.
Willingness to pay	Willingness to pay refers to the largest amount of money that an individual or group could pay, along with a change in policy, without being made worse off.
Substitute good	In economics, one kind of good (or service) is said to be a substitute good for another kind insofar as the two kinds of goods can be consumed or used in place of one another in at least some of their possible uses.
Convexity	In finance, convexity is a measure of the sensitivity of the price of a bond to changes in interest rates. It is related to the concept of duration.

Go to **Cram101.com** for the Practice Tests for this Chapter.

Utility	Utility refers to the want-satisfying power of a good or service; the satisfaction or pleasure a consumer obtains from the consumption of a good or service.
Preference	The act of a debtor in paying or securing one or more of his creditors in a manner more favorable to them than to other creditors or to the exclusion of such other creditors is a preference. In the absence of statute, a preference is perfectly good, but to be legal it must be bona fide, and not a mere subterfuge of the debtor to secure a future benefit to himself or to prevent the application of his property to his debts.
Utility function	Utility function refers to a function that specifies the utility of a consumer for all combinations goods consumed. Represents both their welfare and their preferences.
Consumption	In Keynesian economics consumption refers to personal consumption expenditure, i.e., the purchase of currently produced goods and services out of income, out of savings (net worth), or from borrowed funds. It refers to that part of disposable income that does not go to saving.
Indifference curve	Indifference curve refers to a means of representing the preferences and well being of consumers. Formally, it is a curve representing the combinations of arguments in a utility function that yield a given level of utility.
Assignment	A transfer of property or some right or interest is referred to as assignment.
Ordinal utility	A dimensionless utility measure used in demand theory. Ordinal utility enables one to state that A is preferred to B, but we cannot say by how much.
Points	Loan origination fees that may be deductible as interest by a buyer of property. A seller of property who pays points reduces the selling price by the amount of the points paid for the buyer.
Complement	A good that is used in conjunction with another good is a complement. For example, cameras and film would complement eachother.
Perfect complements	Two goods with right-angle indifference curves are perfect complements. Complements are products consumed simultaneously.
Production	The creation of finished goods and services using the factors of production: land, labor, capital, entrepreneurship, and knowledge.
Marginal utility	Marginal utility refers to the extra utility a consumer obtains from the consumption of 1 additional unit of a good or service; equal to the change in total utility divided by the change in the quantity consumed.
Economics	The social science dealing with the use of scarce resources to obtain the maximum satisfaction of society's virtually unlimited economic wants is an economics.
Total cost	The sum of fixed cost and variable cost is referred to as total cost.
Household	An economic unit that provides the economy with resources and uses the income received to purchase goods and services that satisfy economic wants is called household.
Marginal rate of substitution	In economics, the marginal rate of substitution is the rate at which consumers are willing to give up units of one good in exchange for more units of another good.
Authority	Authority in agency law, refers to an agent's ability to affect his principal's legal relations with third parties. Also used to refer to an actor's legal power or ability to do something. In addition, sometimes used to refer to a statute, case, or other legal source that justifies a particular result.
Policy	Similar to a script in that a policy can be a less than completely rational decision-making method. Involves the use of a pre-existing set of decision steps for any problem that

Go to **Cram101.com** for the Practice Tests for this Chapter.

presents itself.

Derivative A derivative is a generic term for specific types of investments from which payoffs over time are derived from the performance of assets (such as commodities, shares or bonds), interest rates, exchange rates, or indices (such as a stock market index, consumer price index (CPI) or an index of weather conditions).

Go to **Cram101.com** for the Practice Tests for this Chapter.

Indifference curve	Indifference curve refers to a means of representing the preferences and well being of consumers. Formally, it is a curve representing the combinations of arguments in a utility function that yield a given level of utility.
Budget set	A budget set includes all possible consumption bundles that someone can afford given the prices of goods and the person's income level. The budget set is bounded above by the budget line.
Budget	Budget refers to an account, usually for a year, of the planned expenditures and the expected receipts of an entity. For a government, the receipts are tax revenues.
Preference	The act of a debtor in paying or securing one or more of his creditors in a manner more favorable to them than to other creditors or to the exclusion of such other creditors is a preference. In the absence of statute, a preference is perfectly good, but to be legal it must be bona fide, and not a mere subterfuge of the debtor to secure a future benefit to himself or to prevent the application of his property to his debts.
Budget line	Given an allocation of two goods, the budget line through that allocation is the set of all other allocations of the two goods that someone in a market could arrive at by selling one of the goods for the other.
Consumption	In Keynesian economics consumption refers to personal consumption expenditure, i.e., the purchase of currently produced goods and services out of income, out of savings (net worth), or from borrowed funds. It refers to that part of disposable income that does not go to saving.
Optimum	Optimum refers to the best. Usually refers to a most preferred choice by consumers subject to a budget constraint or a profit maximizing choice by firms or industry subject to a technological constraint.
Slope	The slope of a line in the plane containing the x and y axes is generally represented by the letter m, and is defined as the change in the y coordinate divided by the corresponding change in the x coordinate, between two distinct points on the line.
Rate of exchange	Rate of exchange refers to the price paid in one's own money to acquire 1 unit of a foreign currency; the rate at which the money of one nation is exchanged for the money of another nation.
Exchange	The trade of things of value between buyer and seller so that each is better off after the trade is called the exchange.
Market	A market is, as defined in economics, a social arrangement that allows buyers and sellers to discover information and carry out a voluntary exchange of goods or services.
Consumer demand	Consumer demand or consumption is also known as personal consumption expenditure. It is the largest part of aggregate demand or effective demand at the macroeconomic level.There are two variants of consumption in the aggregate demand model, including induced consumption and autonomous consumption.
Perfect substitute	A good that is regarded by its demanders as identical to another good, so that the elasticity of substitution between them is infinite is referred to as perfect substitute.
Complement	A good that is used in conjunction with another good is a complement. For example, cameras and film would complement eachother.
Purchasing	Purchasing refers to the function in a firm that searches for quality material resources, finds the best suppliers, and negotiates the best price for goods and services.
Perfect complements	Two goods with right-angle indifference curves are perfect complements. Complements are products consumed simultaneously.

Go to **Cram101.com** for the Practice Tests for this Chapter.

Property	Assets defined in the broadest legal sense. Property includes the unrealized receivables of a cash basis taxpayer, but not services rendered.
Utility function	Utility function refers to a function that specifies the utility of a consumer for all combinations goods consumed. Represents both their welfare and their preferences.
Utility	Utility refers to the want-satisfying power of a good or service; the satisfaction or pleasure a consumer obtains from the consumption of a good or service.
Economic environment	The economic environment represents the external conditions under which people are engaged in, and benefit from, economic activity. It includes aspects of economic status, paid employment, and finances.
Marginal rate of substitution	In economics, the marginal rate of substitution is the rate at which consumers are willing to give up units of one good in exchange for more units of another good.
Valuation	In finance, valuation is the process of estimating the market value of a financial asset or liability. They can be done on assets (for example, investments in marketable securities such as stocks, options, business enterprises, or intangible assets such as patents and trademarks) or on liabilities (e.g., Bonds issued by a company).
Venture capitalists	Venture capitalists refer to individuals or companies that invest in new businesses in exchange for partial ownership of those businesses.
Market price	Market price is an economic concept with commonplace familiarity; it is the price that a good or service is offered at, or will fetch, in the marketplace; it is of interest mainly in the study of microeconomics.
Inputs	The inputs used by a firm or an economy are the labor, raw materials, electricity and other resources it uses to produce its outputs.
Policy	Similar to a script in that a policy can be a less than completely rational decision-making method. Involves the use of a pre-existing set of decision steps for any problem that presents itself.
Economics	The social science dealing with the use of scarce resources to obtain the maximum satisfaction of society's virtually unlimited economic wants is an economics.
Margin	A deposit by a buyer in stocks with a seller or a stockbroker, as security to cover fluctuations in the market in reference to stocks that the buyer has purchased but for which he has not paid is a margin. Commodities are also traded on margin.
Consumer theory	Consumer theory is a theory of economics. It relates preferences, indifference curves and budget constraints to consumer demand curves. The mathematical models that make up consumer theory can be used in a constrained optimization problem to estimate the optimal goods bundle for an individual buyer.
Presumption	Presumption refers to a term used to signify that which may be assumed without proof, or taken for granted. It is asserted as a self-evident result of human reason and experience.
Budget constraint	Budget constraint refers to the maximum quantity of goods that could be purchased for a given level of income and a given set of prices.
Revenue	Revenue is a U.S. business term for the amount of money that a company receives from its activities, mostly from sales of products and/or services to customers.
Argument	The discussion by counsel for the respective parties of their contentions on the law and the facts of the case being tried in order to aid the jury in arriving at a correct and just conclusion is called argument.
Variable	A variable is something measured by a number; it is used to analyze what happens to other

Go to **Cram101.com** for the Practice Tests for this Chapter.

things when the size of that number changes.

Yield

The interest rate that equates a future value or an annuity to a given present value is a yield.

Derivative

A derivative is a generic term for specific types of investments from which payoffs over time are derived from the performance of assets (such as commodities, shares or bonds), interest rates, exchange rates, or indices (such as a stock market index, consumer price index (CPI) or an index of weather conditions).

Go to **Cram101.com** for the Practice Tests for this Chapter.

Economic environment	The economic environment represents the external conditions under which people are engaged in, and benefit from, economic activity. It includes aspects of economic status, paid employment, and finances.
Comparative static	The comparison of two equilibria from a static model, usually differing by the effects of a single small change in an exogenous variable is a comparative static.
Consumer theory	Consumer theory is a theory of economics. It relates preferences, indifference curves and budget constraints to consumer demand curves. The mathematical models that make up consumer theory can be used in a constrained optimization problem to estimate the optimal goods bundle for an individual buyer.
Comparative statics	Comparative statics is the comparison of two different equilibrium states, before and after a change in one of the variables. Being a study of statics it compares two different unchanging points, once they have changed. It does not study the motion towards equilibrium, nor the process of the change itself.
Inferior good	Inferior good refers to a good for which the demand falls as income rises. The income elasticity of demand is therefore negative.
Change in demand	Change in demand refers to a change in the quantity demanded of a good or service at every price; a shift of the demand curve to the left or right.
Normal good	A good or service whose consumption increases when income increases and falls when income decreases when price remains constant is referred to as normal good.
Economic theory	Economic theory refers to a statement of a cause-effect relationship; when accepted by all economists, an economic principle.
Consumption	In Keynesian economics consumption refers to personal consumption expenditure, i.e., the purchase of currently produced goods and services out of income, out of savings (net worth), or from borrowed funds. It refers to that part of disposable income that does not go to saving.
Offer curve	Offer curve refers to a curve showing, for a two-good model, the quantity of one good that a country will export for each quantity of the other that it imports.
Budget line	Given an allocation of two goods, the budget line through that allocation is the set of all other allocations of the two goods that someone in a market could arrive at by selling one of the goods for the other.
Budget	Budget refers to an account, usually for a year, of the planned expenditures and the expected receipts of an entity. For a government, the receipts are tax revenues.
Expansion path	Expansion path refers to the locus of those cost-minimizing input combinations that a firm will choose to produce various levels of output .
Slope	The slope of a line in the plane containing the x and y axes is generally represented by the letter m, and is defined as the change in the y coordinate divided by the corresponding change in the x coordinate, between two distinct points on the line.
Indifference curve	Indifference curve refers to a means of representing the preferences and well being of consumers. Formally, it is a curve representing the combinations of arguments in a utility function that yield a given level of utility.
Perfect substitute	A good that is regarded by its demanders as identical to another good, so that the elasticity of substitution between them is infinite is referred to as perfect substitute.
Complement	A good that is used in conjunction with another good is a complement. For example, cameras and film would complement eachother.

Perfect complements	Two goods with right-angle indifference curves are perfect complements. Complements are products consumed simultaneously.
Preference	The act of a debtor in paying or securing one or more of his creditors in a manner more favorable to them than to other creditors or to the exclusion of such other creditors is a preference. In the absence of statute, a preference is perfectly good, but to be legal it must be bona fide, and not a mere subterfuge of the debtor to secure a future benefit to himself or to prevent the application of his property to his debts.
Homothetic	A function of two or more arguments is homothetic if all ratios of its first partial derivatives depend only on the ratios of the arguments and not their levels is called homothetic.
Property	Assets defined in the broadest legal sense. Property includes the unrealized receivables of a cash basis taxpayer, but not services rendered.
Homothetic preferences	Together with identical preferences, this assumption is used for many propositions in trade theory, in order to assure that consumers with different incomes but facing the same prices will demand goods in the same proportions are homothetic preferences.
Income effect	Income effect refers to that portion of the effect of price on quantity demanded that reflects the change in real income due to the price change.
Quantity demanded	The amount of a good or service that buyers desire to purchase at a particular price during some period is a quantity demanded.
Giffen good	Giffen good refers to a good that is so inferior and so heavily consumed at low incomes that the demand for it rises when its price rises.
Purchasing power	The amount of goods that money will buy, usually measured by the CPI is referred to as purchasing power.
Purchasing	Purchasing refers to the function in a firm that searches for quality material resources, finds the best suppliers, and negotiates the best price for goods and services.
Demand curve	Demand curve refers to the graph of quantity demanded as a function of price, normally downward sloping, straight or curved, and drawn with quantity on the horizontal axis and price on the vertical axis.
Auction	A preexisting business model that operates successfully on the Internet by announcing an item for sale and permitting multiple purchasers to bid on them under specified rules and condition is an auction.
Utility function	Utility function refers to a function that specifies the utility of a consumer for all combinations goods consumed. Represents both their welfare and their preferences.
Utility	Utility refers to the want-satisfying power of a good or service; the satisfaction or pleasure a consumer obtains from the consumption of a good or service.
Marginal utility	Marginal utility refers to the extra utility a consumer obtains from the consumption of 1 additional unit of a good or service; equal to the change in total utility divided by the change in the quantity consumed.
Argument	The discussion by counsel for the respective parties of their contentions on the law and the facts of the case being tried in order to aid the jury in arriving at a correct and just conclusion is called argument.
Complementary good	A complementary good refers to a product or service that is used together with another good. When the price of one falls, the demand for the other increases. Cameras and film are considered complementary goods.

Go to **Cram101.com** for the Practice Tests for this Chapter.

Points	Loan origination fees that may be deductible as interest by a buyer of property. A seller of property who pays points reduces the selling price by the amount of the points paid for the buyer.
Willingness to pay	Willingness to pay refers to the largest amount of money that an individual or group could pay, along with a change in policy, without being made worse off.
Budget constraint	Budget constraint refers to the maximum quantity of goods that could be purchased for a given level of income and a given set of prices.
Derivative	A derivative is a generic term for specific types of investments from which payoffs over time are derived from the performance of assets (such as commodities, shares or bonds), interest rates, exchange rates, or indices (such as a stock market index, consumer price index (CPI) or an index of weather conditions).

30

Go to **Cram101.com** for the Practice Tests for this Chapter.

Preference	The act of a debtor in paying or securing one or more of his creditors in a manner more favorable to them than to other creditors or to the exclusion of such other creditors is a preference. In the absence of statute, a preference is perfectly good, but to be legal it must be bona fide, and not a mere subterfuge of the debtor to secure a future benefit to himself or to prevent the application of his property to his debts.
Budget	Budget refers to an account, usually for a year, of the planned expenditures and the expected receipts of an entity. For a government, the receipts are tax revenues.
Revealed preference	Revealed preference refers to the use of the value of expenditure to 'reveal' the preference of a consumer or group of consumers for the bundle of goods they purchase compared to other bundles of equal or smaller value.
Indifference curve	Indifference curve refers to a means of representing the preferences and well being of consumers. Formally, it is a curve representing the combinations of arguments in a utility function that yield a given level of utility.
Budget line	Given an allocation of two goods, the budget line through that allocation is the set of all other allocations of the two goods that someone in a market could arrive at by selling one of the goods for the other.
Budget constraint	Budget constraint refers to the maximum quantity of goods that could be purchased for a given level of income and a given set of prices.
Consumer behavior	Consumer behavior refers to the actions a person takes in purchasing and using products and services, including the mental and social processes that precede and follow these actions.
Economic policy	Economic policy refers to the actions that governments take in the economic field. It covers the systems for setting interest rates and government deficit as well as the labor market, national ownership, and many other areas of government.
Policy	Similar to a script in that a policy can be a less than completely rational decision-making method. Involves the use of a pre-existing set of decision steps for any problem that presents itself.
Weighted average	The weighted average unit cost of the goods available for sale for both cost of goods sold and ending inventory.
Economic environment	The economic environment represents the external conditions under which people are engaged in, and benefit from, economic activity. It includes aspects of economic status, paid employment, and finances.
Economic model	Economic model refers to a simplified picture of economic reality; an abstract generalization.
Economic theory	Economic theory refers to a statement of a cause-effect relationship; when accepted by all economists, an economic principle.
Household	An economic unit that provides the economy with resources and uses the income received to purchase goods and services that satisfy economic wants is called household.
Consumption	In Keynesian economics consumption refers to personal consumption expenditure, i.e., the purchase of currently produced goods and services out of income, out of savings (net worth), or from borrowed funds. It refers to that part of disposable income that does not go to saving.
Nonprofit organization	An organization whose goals do not include making a personal profit for its owners is a nonprofit organization.
Base period	Base period refers to the time period used for comparative analysis; the basis for indexing, e.g., of price change. A base period may be a month, year or average of years.

Welfare	Welfare refers to the economic well being of an individual, group, or economy. For individuals, it is conceptualized by a utility function. For groups, including countries and the world, it is a tricky philosophical concept, since individuals fare differently.
Price index	A measure of the average prices of a group of goods relative to a base year. A typical price index for a vector of quantities q and prices pb, pg in the base and given years respectively would be I = 100 Pgq / Pbq.
Laspeyres price index	A measure of the level of prices based on a fixed basket of goods is called the Laspeyres price index.
Social Security	Social security primarily refers to a field of social welfare concerned with social protection, or protection against socially recognized conditions, including poverty, old age, disability, unemployment, families with children and others.
Sole source	A sole source is a supplier that is the only source for a contract item.
Indexing	Indexing refers to provisions in a law or a contract whereby monetary payments are automatically adjusted whenever a specified price index changes.
Security	Security refers to a claim on the borrower future income that is sold by the borrower to the lender. A security is a type of transferable interest representing financial value.
Base year	The year used as the basis for comparison by a price index such as the CPI. The index for any year is the average of prices for that year compared to the base year; e.g., 110 means that prices are 10% higher than in the base year.
Purchasing power	The amount of goods that money will buy, usually measured by the CPI is referred to as purchasing power.
Purchasing	Purchasing refers to the function in a firm that searches for quality material resources, finds the best suppliers, and negotiates the best price for goods and services.
Relative price	Relative price refers to the price of one thing in terms of another; i.e., the ratio of two prices.
Weak axiom of revealed preference	Weak axiom of revealed preference refers to the assumption that a consumer who reveals strict preference for one bundle of goods over another will not, in other circumstances, reveal their preference for the second over the first.

Giffen good	Giffen good refers to a good that is so inferior and so heavily consumed at low incomes that the demand for it rises when its price rises.
Property	Assets defined in the broadest legal sense. Property includes the unrealized receivables of a cash basis taxpayer, but not services rendered.
Purchasing power	The amount of goods that money will buy, usually measured by the CPI is referred to as purchasing power.
Purchasing	Purchasing refers to the function in a firm that searches for quality material resources, finds the best suppliers, and negotiates the best price for goods and services.
Exchange	The trade of things of value between buyer and seller so that each is better off after the trade is called the exchange.
Substitution effect	The substitution effect is a price change that changes the slope of the budget constraint, but leaves the consumer on the same indifference curve. This effect will always cause the consumer to substitute away from the good that is becoming comparatively more expensive.
Substitute good	In economics, one kind of good (or service) is said to be a substitute good for another kind insofar as the two kinds of goods can be consumed or used in place of one another in at least some of their possible uses.
Market	A market is, as defined in economics, a social arrangement that allows buyers and sellers to discover information and carry out a voluntary exchange of goods or services.
Relative price	Relative price refers to the price of one thing in terms of another; i.e., the ratio of two prices.
Holding	The holding is a court's determination of a matter of law based on the issue presented in the particular case. In other words: under this law, with these facts, this result.
Budget	Budget refers to an account, usually for a year, of the planned expenditures and the expected receipts of an entity. For a government, the receipts are tax revenues.
Budget line	Given an allocation of two goods, the budget line through that allocation is the set of all other allocations of the two goods that someone in a market could arrive at by selling one of the goods for the other.
Slope	The slope of a line in the plane containing the x and y axes is generally represented by the letter m, and is defined as the change in the y coordinate divided by the corresponding change in the x coordinate, between two distinct points on the line.
Consumption	In Keynesian economics consumption refers to personal consumption expenditure, i.e., the purchase of currently produced goods and services out of income, out of savings (net worth), or from borrowed funds. It refers to that part of disposable income that does not go to saving.
Slutsky equation	The Slutsky equation is a mathematical representation that relates Marshallian demand and Hicksian demand. It demonstrates that demand changes due to price changes are a result of the substitution effect and the income effect.
Income effect	Income effect refers to that portion of the effect of price on quantity demanded that reflects the change in real income due to the price change.
Indifference curve	Indifference curve refers to a means of representing the preferences and well being of consumers. Formally, it is a curve representing the combinations of arguments in a utility function that yield a given level of utility.
Inferior good	Inferior good refers to a good for which the demand falls as income rises. The income elasticity of demand is therefore negative.

Normal good	A good or service whose consumption increases when income increases and falls when income decreases when price remains constant is referred to as normal good.
Increase in demand	Increase in demand refers to an increase in the quantity demanded of a good or service at every price; a shift of the demand curve to the right.
Budget set	A budget set includes all possible consumption bundles that someone can afford given the prices of goods and the person's income level. The budget set is bounded above by the budget line.
Change in demand	Change in demand refers to a change in the quantity demanded of a good or service at every price; a shift of the demand curve to the left or right.
Income and substitution effects	Income and substitution effects refer to two analytically different effects that come into play when an individual is faced with a changed price for some good.
Income and substitution	Income and substitution refers to two analytically different effects that come into play when an individual is faced with a changed price for some good. The income effect arises because a change in the price of a good will affect an individual's purchasing power. Even if purchasing power is held constant, however, substitution effects will cause individuals to reallocate their expectations. Substitution effects are reflected in movements along an indifference curve, whereas income effects entail a movement to a different indifference curve.
Consumer theory	Consumer theory is a theory of economics. It relates preferences, indifference curves and budget constraints to consumer demand curves. The mathematical models that make up consumer theory can be used in a constrained optimization problem to estimate the optimal goods bundle for an individual buyer.
Complement	A good that is used in conjunction with another good is a complement. For example, cameras and film would complement eachother.
Revenue	Revenue is a U.S. business term for the amount of money that a company receives from its activities, mostly from sales of products and/or services to customers.
Preference	The act of a debtor in paying or securing one or more of his creditors in a manner more favorable to them than to other creditors or to the exclusion of such other creditors is a preference. In the absence of statute, a preference is perfectly good, but to be legal it must be bona fide, and not a mere subterfuge of the debtor to secure a future benefit to himself or to prevent the application of his property to his debts.
Budget constraint	Budget constraint refers to the maximum quantity of goods that could be purchased for a given level of income and a given set of prices.
Variable	A variable is something measured by a number; it is used to analyze what happens to other things when the size of that number changes.
Rebate	Rebate refers to a sales promotion in which money is returned to the consumer based on proof of purchase.
Production	The creation of finished goods and services using the factors of production: land, labor, capital, entrepreneurship, and knowledge.
Peak	Peak refers to the point in the business cycle when an economic expansion reaches its highest point before turning down. Contrasts with trough.
Users	Users refer to people in the organization who actually use the product or service purchased by the buying center.
Incentive	An incentive is any factor (financial or non-financial) that provides a motive for a

Go to **Cram101.com** for the Practice Tests for this Chapter.

	particular course of action, or counts as a reason for preferring one choice to the alternatives.
Supply	Supply is the aggregate amount of any material good that can be called into being at a certain price point; it comprises one half of the equation of supply and demand. In classical economic theory, a curve representing supply is one of the factors that produce price.
Utility	Utility refers to the want-satisfying power of a good or service; the satisfaction or pleasure a consumer obtains from the consumption of a good or service.
Economics	The social science dealing with the use of scarce resources to obtain the maximum satisfaction of society's virtually unlimited economic wants is an economics.
Quantity demanded	The amount of a good or service that buyers desire to purchase at a particular price during some period is a quantity demanded.
Demand curve	Demand curve refers to the graph of quantity demanded as a function of price, normally downward sloping, straight or curved, and drawn with quantity on the horizontal axis and price on the vertical axis.
Context	The effect of the background under which a message often takes on more and richer meaning is a context. Context is especially important in cross-cultural interactions because some cultures are said to be high context or low context.
Compensated demand curve	In economics, the compensated demand curve shows how the substitution effect influences the number of units of a good the consumer will purchase.
Policy	Similar to a script in that a policy can be a less than completely rational decision-making method. Involves the use of a pre-existing set of decision steps for any problem that presents itself.
Law of demand	Law of demand refers to the principle that, other things equal, an increase in a product's price will reduce the quantity of it demanded, and conversely for a decrease in price.

Labor	People's physical and mental talents and efforts that are used to help produce goods and services are called labor.
Asset	An item of property, such as land, capital, money, a share in ownership, or a claim on others for future payment, such as a bond or a bank deposit is an asset.
Market	A market is, as defined in economics, a social arrangement that allows buyers and sellers to discover information and carry out a voluntary exchange of goods or services.
Endowment	Endowment refers to the amount of something that a person or country simply has, rather than their having somehow to acquire it.
Supply	Supply is the aggregate amount of any material good that can be called into being at a certain price point; it comprises one half of the equation of supply and demand. In classical economic theory, a curve representing supply is one of the factors that produce price.
Budget line	Given an allocation of two goods, the budget line through that allocation is the set of all other allocations of the two goods that someone in a market could arrive at by selling one of the goods for the other.
Budget	Budget refers to an account, usually for a year, of the planned expenditures and the expected receipts of an entity. For a government, the receipts are tax revenues.
Buyer	A buyer refers to a role in the buying center with formal authority and responsibility to select the supplier and negotiate the terms of the contract.
Slope	The slope of a line in the plane containing the x and y axes is generally represented by the letter m, and is defined as the change in the y coordinate divided by the corresponding change in the x coordinate, between two distinct points on the line.
Budget constraint	Budget constraint refers to the maximum quantity of goods that could be purchased for a given level of income and a given set of prices.
Consumption	In Keynesian economics consumption refers to personal consumption expenditure, i.e., the purchase of currently produced goods and services out of income, out of savings (net worth), or from borrowed funds. It refers to that part of disposable income that does not go to saving.
Marginal rate of substitution	In economics, the marginal rate of substitution is the rate at which consumers are willing to give up units of one good in exchange for more units of another good.
Relative price	Relative price refers to the price of one thing in terms of another; i.e., the ratio of two prices.
Budget set	A budget set includes all possible consumption bundles that someone can afford given the prices of goods and the person's income level. The budget set is bounded above by the budget line.
Free market	A free market is a market where price is determined by the unregulated interchange of supply and demand rather than set by artificial means.
Consumption possibilities	The alternative combinations of goods and services that a country could consume in a given time period are consumption possibilities.
Preference	The act of a debtor in paying or securing one or more of his creditors in a manner more favorable to them than to other creditors or to the exclusion of such other creditors is a preference. In the absence of statute, a preference is perfectly good, but to be legal it must be bona fide, and not a mere subterfuge of the debtor to secure a future benefit to himself or to prevent the application of his property to his debts.
Revealed	Revealed preference refers to the use of the value of expenditure to 'reveal' the preference

Go to **Cram101.com** for the Practice Tests for this Chapter.

preference	of a consumer or group of consumers for the bundle of goods they purchase compared to other bundles of equal or smaller value.
Points	Loan origination fees that may be deductible as interest by a buyer of property. A seller of property who pays points reduces the selling price by the amount of the points paid for the buyer.
Quantity demanded	The amount of a good or service that buyers desire to purchase at a particular price during some period is a quantity demanded.
Demand curve	Demand curve refers to the graph of quantity demanded as a function of price, normally downward sloping, straight or curved, and drawn with quantity on the horizontal axis and price on the vertical axis.
Offer curve	Offer curve refers to a curve showing, for a two-good model, the quantity of one good that a country will export for each quantity of the other that it imports.
Indifference curve	Indifference curve refers to a means of representing the preferences and well being of consumers. Formally, it is a curve representing the combinations of arguments in a utility function that yield a given level of utility.
Supply curve	Supply curve refers to the graph of quantity supplied as a function of price, normally upward sloping, straight or curved, and drawn with quantity on the horizontal axis and price on the vertical axis.
Property	Assets defined in the broadest legal sense. Property includes the unrealized receivables of a cash basis taxpayer, but not services rendered.
Slutsky equation	The Slutsky equation is a mathematical representation that relates Marshallian demand and Hicksian demand. It demonstrates that demand changes due to price changes are a result of the substitution effect and the income effect.
Change in demand	Change in demand refers to a change in the quantity demanded of a good or service at every price; a shift of the demand curve to the left or right.
Income effect	Income effect refers to that portion of the effect of price on quantity demanded that reflects the change in real income due to the price change.
Substitution effect	The substitution effect is a price change that changes the slope of the budget constraint, but leaves the consumer on the same indifference curve. This effect will always cause the consumer to substitute away from the good that is becoming comparatively more expensive.
Purchasing power	The amount of goods that money will buy, usually measured by the CPI is referred to as purchasing power.
Purchasing	Purchasing refers to the function in a firm that searches for quality material resources, finds the best suppliers, and negotiates the best price for goods and services.
Normal good	A good or service whose consumption increases when income increases and falls when income decreases when price remains constant is referred to as normal good.
Labor supply	The number of workers available to an economy. The principal determinants of labor supply are population, real wages, and social traditions.
Variable	A variable is something measured by a number; it is used to analyze what happens to other things when the size of that number changes.
Wage	The payment for the service of a unit of labor, per unit time. In trade theory, it is the only payment to labor, usually unskilled labor. In empirical work, wage data may exclude other compenzation, which must be added to get the total cost of employment.
Opportunity cost	The cost of something in terms of opportunity foregone. The opportunity cost to a country of

producing a unit more of a good, such as for export or to replace an import, is the quantity of some other good that could have been produced instead.

Exchange	The trade of things of value between buyer and seller so that each is better off after the trade is called the exchange.
Real wage	The wage of labor -- or more generally the price of any factor -- relative to an appropriate price index for the goods and services that the worker consumes is referred to as real wage.
Tradeoff	The sacrifice of some or all of one economic goal, good, or service to achieve some other goal, good, or service is a tradeoff.
Comparative static	The comparison of two equilibria from a static model, usually differing by the effects of a single small change in an exogenous variable is a comparative static.
Comparative statics	Comparative statics is the comparison of two different equilibrium states, before and after a change in one of the variables. Being a study of statics it compares two different unchanging points, once they have changed. It does not study the motion towards equilibrium, nor the process of the change itself.
Income and substitution effects	Income and substitution effects refer to two analytically different effects that come into play when an individual is faced with a changed price for some good.
Income and substitution	Income and substitution refers to two analytically different effects that come into play when an individual is faced with a changed price for some good. The income effect arises because a change in the price of a good will affect an individual's purchasing power. Even if purchasing power is held constant, however, substitution effects will cause individuals to reallocate their expectations. Substitution effects are reflected in movements along an indifference curve, whereas income effects entail a movement to a different indifference curve.
Supply of labor	Supply of labor refers to the relationship between the quantity of labor supplied by employees and the real wage rate when all other influences on work plans remain the same.
Consumer demand	Consumer demand or consumption is also known as personal consumption expenditure. It is the largest part of aggregate demand or effective demand at the macroeconomic level. There are two variants of consumption in the aggregate demand model, including induced consumption and autonomous consumption.
Argument	The discussion by counsel for the respective parties of their contentions on the law and the facts of the case being tried in order to aid the jury in arriving at a correct and just conclusion is called argument.
Overtime	Overtime is the amount of time someone works beyond normal working hours.
Production	The creation of finished goods and services using the factors of production: land, labor, capital, entrepreneurship, and knowledge.
Domestic	From or in one's own country. A domestic producer is one that produces inside the home country. A domestic price is the price inside the home country. Opposite of 'foreign' or 'world.'.
Derivative	A derivative is a generic term for specific types of investments from which payoffs over time are derived from the performance of assets (such as commodities, shares or bonds), interest rates, exchange rates, or indices (such as a stock market index, consumer price index (CPI) or an index of weather conditions).

Intertemporal	Occurring across time, or across different periods of time are intertemporal. Intertemporal choice is essentially the question of whether you consume something now or in the future, this is a form of delayed gratification.
Consumption	In Keynesian economics consumption refers to personal consumption expenditure, i.e., the purchase of currently produced goods and services out of income, out of savings (net worth), or from borrowed funds. It refers to that part of disposable income that does not go to saving.
Budget constraint	Budget constraint refers to the maximum quantity of goods that could be purchased for a given level of income and a given set of prices.
Budget	Budget refers to an account, usually for a year, of the planned expenditures and the expected receipts of an entity. For a government, the receipts are tax revenues.
Interest	In finance and economics, interest is the price paid by a borrower for the use of a lender's money. In other words, interest is the amount of paid to "rent" money for a period of time.
Lender	Suppliers and financial institutions that lend money to companies is referred to as a lender.
Present value	The value today of a stream of payments and/or receipts over time in the future and/or the past, converted to the present using an interest rate. If X t is the amount in period t and r the interest rate, then present value at time t=0 is V = ?T /t.
Future value	Future value measures what money is worth at a specified time in the future assuming a certain interest rate. This is used in time value of money calculations.
Budget set	A budget set includes all possible consumption bundles that someone can afford given the prices of goods and the person's income level. The budget set is bounded above by the budget line.
Endowment	Endowment refers to the amount of something that a person or country simply has, rather than their having somehow to acquire it.
Intertemporal budget constraint	The budget constraint applying to expenditure and income in more than one period of time is referred to as an intertemporal budget constraint.
Indifference curve	Indifference curve refers to a means of representing the preferences and well being of consumers. Formally, it is a curve representing the combinations of arguments in a utility function that yield a given level of utility.
Slope	The slope of a line in the plane containing the x and y axes is generally represented by the letter m, and is defined as the change in the y coordinate divided by the corresponding change in the x coordinate, between two distinct points on the line.
Marginal rate of substitution	In economics, the marginal rate of substitution is the rate at which consumers are willing to give up units of one good in exchange for more units of another good.
Complement	A good that is used in conjunction with another good is a complement. For example, cameras and film would complement eachother.
Perfect complements	Two goods with right-angle indifference curves are perfect complements. Complements are products consumed simultaneously.
Preference	The act of a debtor in paying or securing one or more of his creditors in a manner more favorable to them than to other creditors or to the exclusion of such other creditors is a preference. In the absence of statute, a preference is perfectly good, but to be legal it must be bona fide, and not a mere subterfuge of the debtor to secure a future benefit to himself or to prevent the application of his property to his debts.

Convexity	In finance, convexity is a measure of the sensitivity of the price of a bond to changes in interest rates. It is related to the concept of duration.
Context	The effect of the background under which a message often takes on more and richer meaning is a context. Context is especially important in cross-cultural interactions because some cultures are said to be high context or low context.
Comparative static	The comparison of two equilibria from a static model, usually differing by the effects of a single small change in an exogenous variable is a comparative static.
Comparative statics	Comparative statics is the comparison of two different equilibrium states, before and after a change in one of the variables. Being a study of statics it compares two different unchanging points, once they have changed. It does not study the motion towards equilibrium, nor the process of the change itself.
Interest rate	The rate of return on bonds, loans, or deposits. When one speaks of 'the' interest rate, it is usually in a model where there is only one.
Budget line	Given an allocation of two goods, the budget line through that allocation is the set of all other allocations of the two goods that someone in a market could arrive at by selling one of the goods for the other.
Revealed preference	Revealed preference refers to the use of the value of expenditure to 'reveal' the preference of a consumer or group of consumers for the bundle of goods they purchase compared to other bundles of equal or smaller value.
Welfare	Welfare refers to the economic well being of an individual, group, or economy. For individuals, it is conceptualized by a utility function. For groups, including countries and the world, it is a tricky philosophical concept, since individuals fare differently.
Change in demand	Change in demand refers to a change in the quantity demanded of a good or service at every price; a shift of the demand curve to the left or right.
Slutsky equation	The Slutsky equation is a mathematical representation that relates Marshallian demand and Hicksian demand. It demonstrates that demand changes due to price changes are a result of the substitution effect and the income effect.
Income effect	Income effect refers to that portion of the effect of price on quantity demanded that reflects the change in real income due to the price change.
Substitution effect	The substitution effect is a price change that changes the slope of the budget constraint, but leaves the consumer on the same indifference curve. This effect will always cause the consumer to substitute away from the good that is becoming comparatively more expensive.
Normal good	A good or service whose consumption increases when income increases and falls when income decreases when price remains constant is referred to as normal good.
Inflation	An increase in the overall price level of an economy, usually as measured by the CPI or by the implicit price deflator is called inflation.
Deflation	Deflation is an increase in the market value of money which is equivalent to a decrease in the general price level, over a period of time. The term is also used to refer to a decrease in the size of the money supply
Inflation rate	The percentage increase in the price level per year is an inflation rate. Alternatively, the inflation rate is the rate of decrease in the purchasing power of money.
Real rate of interest	The real rate of interest is the percentage increase in purchasing power that the borrower pays to the lender for the privilege of borrowing. It is the nominal rate of interest minus the inflation rate.

51

Nominal rate of interest	The nominal rate of interest is the percentage by which the money the borrower pays back exceeds the money that he borrowed, making no adjustment for any fall in the purchasing power of this money that results from inflation.
Real interest rate	The real interest rate is the nominal interest rate minus the inflation rate. It is a better measure of the return that a lender receives (or the cost to the borrower) because it takes into account the fact that the value of money changes due to inflation over the course of the loan period.
Consumption possibilities	The alternative combinations of goods and services that a country could consume in a given time period are consumption possibilities.
Investment	Investment refers to spending for the production and accumulation of capital and additions to inventories. In a financial sense, buying an asset with the expectation of making a return.
Yield	The interest rate that equates a future value or an annuity to a given present value is a yield.
Market	A market is, as defined in economics, a social arrangement that allows buyers and sellers to discover information and carry out a voluntary exchange of goods or services.
Net present value	Net present value is a standard method in finance of capital budgeting – the planning of long-term investments. Using this method a potential investment project should be undertaken if the present value of all cash inflows minus the present value of all cash outflows (which equals the net present value) is greater than zero.
Cash flow	In finance, cash flow refers to the amounts of cash being received and spent by a business during a defined period of time, sometimes tied to a specific project. Most of the time they are being used to determine gaps in the liquid position of a company.
Discount	The difference between the face value of a bond and its selling price, when a bond is sold for less than its face value it's referred to as a discount.
Credit	Credit refers to a recording as positive in the balance of payments, any transaction that gives rise to a payment into the country, such as an export, the sale of an asset, or borrowing from abroad.
Balance	In banking and accountancy, the outstanding balance is the amount of money owned, (or due), that remains in a deposit account (or a loan account) at a given date, after all past remittances, payments and withdrawal have been accounted for. It can be positive (then, in the balance sheet of a firm, it is an asset) or negative (a liability).
Instrument	Instrument refers to an economic variable that is controlled by policy makers and can be used to influence other variables, called targets. Examples are monetary and fiscal policies used to achieve external and internal balance.
Security	Security refers to a claim on the borrower future income that is sold by the borrower to the lender. A security is a type of transferable interest representing financial value.
Bond	Bond refers to a debt instrument, issued by a borrower and promising a specified stream of payments to the purchaser, usually regular interest payments plus a final repayment of principal.
Financial instrument	Formal or legal documents in writing, such as contracts, deeds, wills, bonds, leases, and mortgages is referred to as a financial instrument.
Financial market	In economics, a financial market is a mechanism which allows people to trade money for securities or commodities such as gold or other precious metals. In general, any commodity market might be considered to be a financial market, if the usual purpose of traders is not the immediate consumption of the commodity, but rather as a means of delaying or accelerating

Go to **Cram101.com** for the Practice Tests for this Chapter.

consumption over time.

Corporation	A legal entity chartered by a state or the Federal government that is distinct and separate from the individuals who own it is a corporation. This separation gives the corporation unique powers which other legal entities lack.
Maturity date	The date on which the final payment on a bond is due from the bond issuer to the investor is a maturity date.
Face value	The nominal or par value of an instrument as expressed on its face is referred to as the face value.
Maturity	Maturity refers to the final payment date of a loan or other financial instrument, after which point no further interest or principal need be paid.
Coupon	In finance, a coupon is "attached" to a bond, either physically (as with old bonds) or electronically. Each coupon represents a predetermined payment promized to the bond-holder in return for his or her loan of money to the bond-issuer. .
Holder	A person in possession of a document of title or an instrument payable or indorsed to him, his order, or to bearer is a holder.
Agent	A person who makes economic decisions for another economic actor. A hired manager operates as an agent for a firm's owner.
Market value	Market value refers to the price of an asset agreed on between a willing buyer and a willing seller; the price an asset could demand if it is sold on the open market.
Consol	A perpetual bond with no maturity date and no repayment of principal that periodically makes fixed coupon payments is called a consol.
Interest payment	The payment to holders of bonds payable, calculated by multiplying the stated rate on the face of the bond by the par, or face, value of the bond. If bonds are issued at a discount or premium, the interest payment does not equal the interest expense.
Deductible	The dollar sum of costs that an insured individual must pay before the insurer begins to pay is called deductible.
Subsidy	Subsidy refers to government financial assistance to a domestic producer.
Aid	Assistance provided by countries and by international institutions such as the World Bank to developing countries in the form of monetary grants, loans at low interest rates, in kind, or a combination of these is called aid. Aid can also refer to assistance of any type rendered to benefit some group or individual.
Expense	In accounting, an expense represents an event in which an asset is used up or a liability is incurred. In terms of the accounting equation, expenses reduce owners' equity.
Asset	An item of property, such as land, capital, money, a share in ownership, or a claim on others for future payment, such as a bond or a bank deposit is an asset.
Contribution	In business organization law, the cash or property contributed to a business by its owners is referred to as contribution.
Economics	The social science dealing with the use of scarce resources to obtain the maximum satisfaction of society's virtually unlimited economic wants is an economics.
Interest income	Interest income refers to payments of income to those who supply the economy with capital.
Household	An economic unit that provides the economy with resources and uses the income received to purchase goods and services that satisfy economic wants is called household.
Present	Present discounted value refers to present value. It is based on the premise that person

Go to **Cram101.com** for the Practice Tests for this Chapter.

discounted value	prefers to receive a certain amount of money today, rather than the same amount in the future, all else equal.
Fund	Independent accounting entity with a self-balancing set of accounts segregated for the purposes of carrying on specific activities is referred to as a fund.
Property	Assets defined in the broadest legal sense. Property includes the unrealized receivables of a cash basis taxpayer, but not services rendered.
Opportunity cost	The cost of something in terms of opportunity foregone. The opportunity cost to a country of producing a unit more of a good, such as for export or to replace an import, is the quantity of some other good that could have been produced instead.
Intertemporal consumption	Economic theories of intertemporal consumption seek to explain people's preferences in relation to consumption and saving over the course of their life. The earliest work on the subject was by Irving Fisher and Roy Harrod who described 'hump saving', hypothesizing that savings would be highest in the middle years of a person's life as they saved for retirement.

Consumption	In Keynesian economics consumption refers to personal consumption expenditure, i.e., the purchase of currently produced goods and services out of income, out of savings (net worth), or from borrowed funds. It refers to that part of disposable income that does not go to saving.
Service	Service refers to a "non tangible product" that is not embodied in a physical good and that typically effects some change in another product, person, or institution. Contrasts with good.
Asset	An item of property, such as land, capital, money, a share in ownership, or a claim on others for future payment, such as a bond or a bank deposit is an asset.
Financial assets	Financial assets refer to monetary claims or obligations by one party against another party. Examples are bonds, mortgages, bank loans, and equities.
Interest payment	The payment to holders of bonds payable, calculated by multiplying the stated rate on the face of the bond by the par, or face, value of the bond. If bonds are issued at a discount or premium, the interest payment does not equal the interest expense.
Interest	In finance and economics, interest is the price paid by a borrower for the use of a lender's money. In other words, interest is the amount of paid to "rent" money for a period of time.
Rate of return	A rate of return is a comparison of the money earned (or lost) on an investment to the amount of money invested.
Cash flow	In finance, cash flow refers to the amounts of cash being received and spent by a business during a defined period of time, sometimes tied to a specific project. Most of the time they are being used to determine gaps in the liquid position of a company.
Future value	Future value measures what money is worth at a specified time in the future assuming a certain interest rate. This is used in time value of money calculations.
Operation	A standardized method or technique that is performed repetitively, often on different materials resulting in different finished goods is called an operation.
Arbitrage	An arbitrage is a combination of nearly simultaneous transactions designed to profit from an existing discrepancy among prices, exchange rates, and/or interest rates on different markets without assuming risk.
Market	A market is, as defined in economics, a social arrangement that allows buyers and sellers to discover information and carry out a voluntary exchange of goods or services.
Supply	Supply is the aggregate amount of any material good that can be called into being at a certain price point; it comprises one half of the equation of supply and demand. In classical economic theory, a curve representing supply is one of the factors that produce price.
Present value	The value today of a stream of payments and/or receipts over time in the future and/or the past, converted to the present using an interest rate. If X_t is the amount in period t and r the interest rate, then present value at time t=0 is $V = ?T /t$.
Privilege	Generally, a legal right to engage in conduct that would otherwise result in legal liability is a privilege. Privileges are commonly classified as absolute or conditional. Occasionally, privilege is also used to denote a legal right to refrain from particular behavior.
Open market	In economics, the open market is the term used to refer to the environment in which bonds are bought and sold.
Opportunity cost	The cost of something in terms of opportunity foregone. The opportunity cost to a country of producing a unit more of a good, such as for export or to replace an import, is the quantity of some other good that could have been produced instead.

Go to **Cram101.com** for the Practice Tests for this Chapter.

Investment	Investment refers to spending for the production and accumulation of capital and additions to inventories. In a financial sense, buying an asset with the expectation of making a return.
Estate	An estate is the totality of the legal rights, interests, entitlements and obligations attaching to property. In the context of wills and probate, it refers to the totality of the property which the deceased owned or in which some interest was held.
Agent	A person who makes economic decisions for another economic actor. A hired manager operates as an agent for a firm's owner.
Revenue	Revenue is a U.S. business term for the amount of money that a company receives from its activities, mostly from sales of products and/or services to customers.
Internal Revenue Service	In 1862, during the Civil War, President Lincoln and Congress created the office of Commissioner of Internal Revenue and enacted an income tax to pay war expenses. The position of Commissioner still exists today. The Commissioner is the head of the Internal Revenue Service.
Capital gain	Capital gain refers to the gain in value that the owner of an asset experiences when the price of the asset rises, including when the currency in which the asset is denominated appreciates.
Capital	Capital generally refers to financial wealth, especially that used to start or maintain a business. In classical economics, capital is one of four factors of production, the others being land and labor and entrepreneurship.
Gain	In finance, gain is a profit or an increase in value of an investment such as a stock or bond. Gain is calculated by fair market value or the proceeds from the sale of the investment minus the sum of the purchase price and all costs associated with it.
Policy	Similar to a script in that a policy can be a less than completely rational decision-making method. Involves the use of a pre-existing set of decision steps for any problem that presents itself.
Effective tax rate	The effective tax rate is the amount of income tax an individual or firm pays divided by the individual or firm's total taxable income. This ratio is usually expressed as a percentage.
Real value	Real value is the value of anything expressed in money of the day with the effects of inflation removed.
Inflation	An increase in the overall price level of an economy, usually as measured by the CPI or by the implicit price deflator is called inflation.
Dividend	Amount of corporate profits paid out for each share of stock is referred to as dividend.
Holding	The holding is a court's determination of a matter of law based on the issue presented in the particular case. In other words: under this law, with these facts, this result.
Argument	The discussion by counsel for the respective parties of their contentions on the law and the facts of the case being tried in order to aid the jury in arriving at a correct and just conclusion is called argument.
Price level	The overall level of prices in a country, as usually measured empirically by a price index, but often captured in theoretical models by a single variable is a price level.
Technology	The body of knowledge and techniques that can be used to combine economic resources to produce goods and services is called technology.
Perfect substitute	A good that is regarded by its demanders as identical to another good, so that the elasticity of substitution between them is infinite is referred to as perfect substitute.
Interest rate	The rate of return on bonds, loans, or deposits. When one speaks of 'the' interest rate, it

Go to **Cram101.com** for the Practice Tests for this Chapter.

is usually in a model where there is only one.

United Nations	An international organization created by multilateral treaty in 1945 to promote social and economic cooperation among nations and to protect human rights is the United Nations.
Profit	Profit refers to the return to the resource entrepreneurial ability; total revenue minus total cost.
Firm	An organization that employs resources to produce a good or service for profit and owns and operates one or more plants is referred to as a firm.
Financial institution	A financial institution acts as an agent that provides financial services for its clients. Financial institutions generally fall under financial regulation from a government authority.
Scarcity	Scarcity is defined as not having sufficient resources to produce enough to fulfill unlimited subjective wants. Alternatively, scarcity implies that not all of society's goals can be attained at the same time, so that trade-offs one good against others are made.
Market economy	A market economy is an economic system in which the production and distribution of goods and services takes place through the mechanism of free markets guided by a free price system rather than by the state in a planned economy.
World price	The price of a good on the 'world market,' meaning the price outside of any country's borders and therefore exclusive of any trade taxes or subsidies is the world price.
Economy	The income, expenditures, and resources that affect the cost of running a business and household are called an economy.
Production	The creation of finished goods and services using the factors of production: land, labor, capital, entrepreneurship, and knowledge.
Preference	The act of a debtor in paying or securing one or more of his creditors in a manner more favorable to them than to other creditors or to the exclusion of such other creditors is a preference. In the absence of statute, a preference is perfectly good, but to be legal it must be bona fide, and not a mere subterfuge of the debtor to secure a future benefit to himself or to prevent the application of his property to his debts.
Endowment	Endowment refers to the amount of something that a person or country simply has, rather than their having somehow to acquire it.
Mortgage	Mortgage refers to a note payable issued for property, such as a house, usually repaid in equal installments consisting of part principle and part interest, over a specified period.
Entrepreneur	The owner/operator. The person who organizes, manages, and assumes the risks of a firm, taking a new idea or a new product and turning it into a successful business is an entrepreneur.
Shares	Shares refer to an equity security, representing a shareholder's ownership of a corporation. Shares are one of a finite number of equal portions in the capital of a company, entitling the owner to a proportion of distributed, non-reinvested profits known as dividends and to a portion of the value of the company in case of liquidation.
Intertemporal	Occurring across time, or across different periods of time are intertemporal. Intertemporal choice is essentially the question of whether you consume something now or in the future, this is a form of delayed gratification.
Intertemporal trade	Trade across time, as when a country imports in one time period paying for the imports with exports in a different time period, earlier or later. And imbalance in the balance of trade is presumed to reflect intertemporal trade.
Municipal bond	In the United States, a municipal bond is a bond issued by a state, city or other local

government, or their agencies. Potential issuers of these include cities, counties, redevelopment agencies, school districts, publicly owned airports and seaports, and any other governmental entity (or group of governments) below the state level. They are guaranteed by a local government, a subdivision thereof, or a group of local governments, and are assessed for risk and rated accordingly.

Bond

Bond refers to a debt instrument, issued by a borrower and promising a specified stream of payments to the purchaser, usually regular interest payments plus a final repayment of principal.

64

Go to **Cram101.com** for the Practice Tests for this Chapter.

Investment	Investment refers to spending for the production and accumulation of capital and additions to inventories. In a financial sense, buying an asset with the expectation of making a return.
Consumption	In Keynesian economics consumption refers to personal consumption expenditure, i.e., the purchase of currently produced goods and services out of income, out of savings (net worth), or from borrowed funds. It refers to that part of disposable income that does not go to saving.
Distribution	Distribution in economics, the manner in which total output and income is distributed among individuals or factors.
Probability distribution	A specification of the probabilities for each possible value of a random variable is called probability distribution.
Insurance	Insurance refers to a system by which individuals can reduce their exposure to risk of large losses by spreading the risks among a large number of persons.
Stock market	An organized marketplace in which common stocks are traded. In the United States, the largest stock market is the New York Stock Exchange, on which are traded the stocks of the largest U.S. companies.
Market	A market is, as defined in economics, a social arrangement that allows buyers and sellers to discover information and carry out a voluntary exchange of goods or services.
Stock	In financial terminology, stock is the capital raized by a corporation, through the issuance and sale of shares.
Endowment	Endowment refers to the amount of something that a person or country simply has, rather than their having somehow to acquire it.
Premium	Premium refers to the fee charged by an insurance company for an insurance policy. The rate of losses must be relatively predictable: In order to set the premium (prices) insurers must be able to estimate them accurately.
Asset	An item of property, such as land, capital, money, a share in ownership, or a claim on others for future payment, such as a bond or a bank deposit is an asset.
Preference	The act of a debtor in paying or securing one or more of his creditors in a manner more favorable to them than to other creditors or to the exclusion of such other creditors is a preference. In the absence of statute, a preference is perfectly good, but to be legal it must be bona fide, and not a mere subterfuge of the debtor to secure a future benefit to himself or to prevent the application of his property to his debts.
Contract	A contract is a "promise" or an "agreement" that is enforced or recognized by the law. In the civil law, a contract is considered to be part of the general law of obligations.
Budget line	Given an allocation of two goods, the budget line through that allocation is the set of all other allocations of the two goods that someone in a market could arrive at by selling one of the goods for the other.
Budget	Budget refers to an account, usually for a year, of the planned expenditures and the expected receipts of an entity. For a government, the receipts are tax revenues.
Exchange	The trade of things of value between buyer and seller so that each is better off after the trade is called the exchange.
Consumption possibilities	The alternative combinations of goods and services that a country could consume in a given time period are consumption possibilities.
Indifference curve	Indifference curve refers to a means of representing the preferences and well being of consumers. Formally, it is a curve representing the combinations of arguments in a utility

function that yield a given level of utility.

Marginal rate of substitution	In economics, the marginal rate of substitution is the rate at which consumers are willing to give up units of one good in exchange for more units of another good.
Consumer behavior	Consumer behavior refers to the actions a person takes in purchasing and using products and services, including the mental and social processes that precede and follow these actions.
Catastrophe bond	Catastrophe bonds (also known as cat bonds) are risk-linked securities that transfer a specified set of risks from the sponsor to the investors. They are often structured as floating-rate corporate bonds whose principal is forgiven if specified trigger conditions are met. They are typically used by insurers as an alternative to traditional catastrophe reinsurance.
Bond	Bond refers to a debt instrument, issued by a borrower and promising a specified stream of payments to the purchaser, usually regular interest payments plus a final repayment of principal.
Wholesale	According to the United Nations Statistics Division Wholesale is the resale of new and used goods to retailers, to industrial, commercial, institutional or professional users, or to other wholesalers, or involves acting as an agent or broker in buying merchandise for, or selling merchandise, to such persons or companies.
Buyer	A buyer refers to a role in the buying center with formal authority and responsibility to select the supplier and negotiate the terms of the contract.
Reinsurance	An allocation of the portion of the insurance risk to another company in exchange for a portion of the insurance premium is called reinsurance.
Pension fund	Amounts of money put aside by corporations, nonprofit organizations, or unions to cover part of the financial needs of members when they retire is a pension fund.
Pension	A pension is a steady income given to a person (usually after retirement). Pensions are typically payments made in the form of a guaranteed annuity to a retired or disabled employee.
Fund	Independent accounting entity with a self-balancing set of accounts segregated for the purposes of carrying on specific activities is referred to as a fund.
Consortia	B2B marketplaces sponsored by a group of otherwise competitive enterprises in a specific industry like automobile manufacturing or airline operations are called a consortia.
Industry	A group of firms that produce identical or similar products is an industry. It is also used specifically to refer to an area of economic production focused on manufacturing which involves large amounts of capital investment before any profit can be realized, also called "heavy industry".
Financial intermediary	Financial intermediary refers to a financial institution, such as a bank or a life insurance company, which directs other people's money into such investments as government and corporate securities.
Interest rate	The rate of return on bonds, loans, or deposits. When one speaks of 'the' interest rate, it is usually in a model where there is only one.
Interest	In finance and economics, interest is the price paid by a borrower for the use of a lender's money. In other words, interest is the amount of paid to "rent" money for a period of time.
Default risk	The chance that the issuer of a debt instrument will be unable to make interest payments or pay off the face value when the instrument matures is called default risk.
Default	In finance, default occurs when a debtor has not met its legal obligations according to the

Go to **Cram101.com** for the Practice Tests for this Chapter.
And, **NEVER** highlight a book again!

debt contract, e.g. it has not made a scheduled payment, or violated a covenant (condition) of the debt contract.

Security
Security refers to a claim on the borrower future income that is sold by the borrower to the lender. A security is a type of transferable interest representing financial value.

Derivative
A derivative is a generic term for specific types of investments from which payoffs over time are derived from the performance of assets (such as commodities, shares or bonds), interest rates, exchange rates, or indices (such as a stock market index, consumer price index (CPI) or an index of weather conditions).

Utility function
Utility function refers to a function that specifies the utility of a consumer for all combinations goods consumed. Represents both their welfare and their preferences.

Utility
Utility refers to the want-satisfying power of a good or service; the satisfaction or pleasure a consumer obtains from the consumption of a good or service.

Context
The effect of the background under which a message often takes on more and richer meaning is a context. Context is especially important in cross-cultural interactions because some cultures are said to be high context or low context.

Perfect substitute
A good that is regarded by its demanders as identical to another good, so that the elasticity of substitution between them is infinite is referred to as perfect substitute.

Expected value
A representative value from a probability distribution arrived at by multiplying each outcome by the associated probability and summing up the values is called the expected value.

Property
Assets defined in the broadest legal sense. Property includes the unrealized receivables of a cash basis taxpayer, but not services rendered.

Game theory
The modeling of strategic interactions among agents, used in economic models where the numbers of interacting agents is small enough that each has a perceptible influence on the others is called game theory.

Risk aversion
Risk aversion is the reluctance of a person to accept a bargain with an uncertain payoff rather than another bargain with a more certain but possibly lower expected payoff.

Slope
The slope of a line in the plane containing the x and y axes is generally represented by the letter m, and is defined as the change in the y coordinate divided by the corresponding change in the x coordinate, between two distinct points on the line.

Marginal utility
Marginal utility refers to the extra utility a consumer obtains from the consumption of 1 additional unit of a good or service; equal to the change in total utility divided by the change in the quantity consumed.

Holding
The holding is a court's determination of a matter of law based on the issue presented in the particular case. In other words: under this law, with these facts, this result.

Ford
Ford is an American company that manufactures and sells automobiles worldwide. Ford introduced methods for large-scale manufacturing of cars, and large-scale management of an industrial workforce, especially elaborately engineered manufacturing sequences typified by the moving assembly lines.

Cooperative
A business owned and controlled by the people who use it, producers, consumers, or workers with similar needs who pool their resources for mutual gain is called cooperative.

Firm
An organization that employs resources to produce a good or service for profit and owns and operates one or more plants is referred to as a firm.

Enterprise
Enterprise refers to another name for a business organization. Other similar terms are business firm, sometimes simply business, sometimes simply firm, as well as company, and

Go to **Cram101.com** for the Practice Tests for this Chapter.

entity.

Shareholder	A shareholder is an individual or company (including a corporation) that legally owns one or more shares of stock in a joined stock company.
Incentive	An incentive is any factor (financial or non-financial) that provides a motive for a particular course of action, or counts as a reason for preferring one choice to the alternatives.
Shares	Shares refer to an equity security, representing a shareholder's ownership of a corporation. Shares are one of a finite number of equal portions in the capital of a company, entitling the owner to a proportion of distributed, non-reinvested profits known as dividends and to a portion of the value of the company in case of liquidation.
Policy	Similar to a script in that a policy can be a less than completely rational decision-making method. Involves the use of a pre-existing set of decision steps for any problem that presents itself.
Purchasing	Purchasing refers to the function in a firm that searches for quality material resources, finds the best suppliers, and negotiates the best price for goods and services.
Financial institution	A financial institution acts as an agent that provides financial services for its clients. Financial institutions generally fall under financial regulation from a government authority.
Expected return	Expected return refers to the return on an asset expected over the next period.
Gain	In finance, gain is a profit or an increase in value of an investment such as a stock or bond. Gain is calculated by fair market value or the proceeds from the sale of the investment minus the sum of the purchase price and all costs associated with it.

Utility	Utility refers to the want-satisfying power of a good or service; the satisfaction or pleasure a consumer obtains from the consumption of a good or service.
Utility function	Utility function refers to a function that specifies the utility of a consumer for all combinations goods consumed. Represents both their welfare and their preferences.
Distribution	Distribution in economics, the manner in which total output and income is distributed among individuals or factors.
Probability distribution	A specification of the probabilities for each possible value of a random variable is called probability distribution.
Variance	Variance refers to a measure of how much an economic or statistical variable varies across values or observations. Its calculation is the same as that of the covariance, being the covariance of the variable with itself.
Standard deviation	A measure of the spread or dispersion of a series of numbers around the expected value is the standard deviation. The standard deviation tells us how well the expected value represents a series of values.
Rate of return	A rate of return is a comparison of the money earned (or lost) on an investment to the amount of money invested.
Asset	An item of property, such as land, capital, money, a share in ownership, or a claim on others for future payment, such as a bond or a bank deposit is an asset.
Mutual fund	A mutual fund is a form of collective investment that pools money from many investors and invests the money in stocks, bonds, short-term money market instruments, and/or other securities. In a mutual fund, the fund manager trades the fund's underlying securities, realizing capital gains or loss, and collects the dividend or interest income.
Investment	Investment refers to spending for the production and accumulation of capital and additions to inventories. In a financial sense, buying an asset with the expectation of making a return.
Stock	In financial terminology, stock is the capital raized by a corporation, through the issuance and sale of shares.
Fund	Independent accounting entity with a self-balancing set of accounts segregated for the purposes of carrying on specific activities is referred to as a fund.
Stock market	An organized marketplace in which common stocks are traded. In the United States, the largest stock market is the New York Stock Exchange, on which are traded the stocks of the largest U.S. companies.
Market	A market is, as defined in economics, a social arrangement that allows buyers and sellers to discover information and carry out a voluntary exchange of goods or services.
Expected return	Expected return refers to the return on an asset expected over the next period.
Portfolio	In finance, a portfolio is a collection of investments held by an institution or a private individual. Holding but not always a portfolio is part of an investment and risk-limiting strategy called diversification. By owning several assets, certain types of risk (in particular specific risk) can be reduced.
Budget line	Given an allocation of two goods, the budget line through that allocation is the set of all other allocations of the two goods that someone in a market could arrive at by selling one of the goods for the other.
Budget	Budget refers to an account, usually for a year, of the planned expenditures and the expected receipts of an entity. For a government, the receipts are tax revenues.
Indifference	Indifference curve refers to a means of representing the preferences and well being of

curve	consumers. Formally, it is a curve representing the combinations of arguments in a utility function that yield a given level of utility.
Points	Loan origination fees that may be deductible as interest by a buyer of property. A seller of property who pays points reduces the selling price by the amount of the points paid for the buyer.
Preference	The act of a debtor in paying or securing one or more of his creditors in a manner more favorable to them than to other creditors or to the exclusion of such other creditors is a preference. In the absence of statute, a preference is perfectly good, but to be legal it must be bona fide, and not a mere subterfuge of the debtor to secure a future benefit to himself or to prevent the application of his property to his debts.
Marginal rate of substitution	In economics, the marginal rate of substitution is the rate at which consumers are willing to give up units of one good in exchange for more units of another good.
Inferior good	Inferior good refers to a good for which the demand falls as income rises. The income elasticity of demand is therefore negative.
Normal good	A good or service whose consumption increases when income increases and falls when income decreases when price remains constant is referred to as normal good.
Revealed preference	Revealed preference refers to the use of the value of expenditure to 'reveal' the preference of a consumer or group of consumers for the bundle of goods they purchase compared to other bundles of equal or smaller value.
Budget set	A budget set includes all possible consumption bundles that someone can afford given the prices of goods and the person's income level. The budget set is bounded above by the budget line.
Argument	The discussion by counsel for the respective parties of their contentions on the law and the facts of the case being tried in order to aid the jury in arriving at a correct and just conclusion is called argument.
Total utility	The total amount of satisfaction derived from the consumption of a single product or a combination of products is total utility.
Economics	The social science dealing with the use of scarce resources to obtain the maximum satisfaction of society's virtually unlimited economic wants is an economics.
Correlation	A correlation is the measure of the extent to which two economic or statistical variables move together, normalized so that its values range from -1 to +1. It is defined as the covariance of the two variables divided by the square root of the product of their variances.
Variable	A variable is something measured by a number; it is used to analyze what happens to other things when the size of that number changes.
Service	Service refers to a "non tangible product" that is not embodied in a physical good and that typically effects some change in another product, person, or institution. Contrasts with good.
Diversified portfolio	Diversified portfolio refers to a portfolio that includes a variety of assets whose prices are not likely all to change together. In international economics, this usually means holding assets denominated in different currencies.
Risk premium	In finance, the risk premium can be the expected rate of return above the risk-free interest rate.
Premium	Premium refers to the fee charged by an insurance company for an insurance policy. The rate of losses must be relatively predictable: In order to set the premium (prices) insurers must be able to estimate them accurately.

77

Expected value	A representative value from a probability distribution arrived at by multiplying each outcome by the associated probability and summing up the values is called the expected value.
Expected rate of return	Expected rate of return refers to the increase in profit a firm anticipates it will obtain by purchasing capital ; expressed as a percentage of the total cost of the investment activity.
Capital asset	In accounting, a capital asset is an asset that is recorded as property that creates more property, e.g. a factory that creates shoes, or a forest that yields a quantity of wood.
Capital	Capital generally refers to financial wealth, especially that used to start or maintain a business. In classical economics, capital is one of four factors of production, the others being land and labor and entrepreneurship.
Capital asset pricing model	The capital asset pricing model is used in finance to determine a theoretically appropriate required rate of return (and thus the price if expected cash flows can be estimated) of an asset, if that asset is to be added to an already well-diversified portfolio, given that asset's non-diversifiable risk.
Profit	Profit refers to the return to the resource entrepreneurial ability; total revenue minus total cost.
Journal	Book of original entry, in which transactions are recorded in a general ledger system, is referred to as a journal.
Holding	The holding is a court's determination of a matter of law based on the issue presented in the particular case. In other words: under this law, with these facts, this result.
Management	Management characterizes the process of leading and directing all or part of an organization, often a business, through the deployment and manipulation of resources. Early twentieth-century management writer Mary Parker Follett defined management as "the art of getting things done through people."
Below the line	Below the line is an advertising technique. It uses less conventional methods than the usual specific channels of advertising to promote products, services, etc. than ATL (Above the line) strategy.
Above the line	Above the line is an advertising technique using mass media to promote brands. This type of communication is conventional in nature and is considered impersonal to customers.
Slope	The slope of a line in the plane containing the x and y axes is generally represented by the letter m, and is defined as the change in the y coordinate divided by the corresponding change in the x coordinate, between two distinct points on the line.

Utility function	Utility function refers to a function that specifies the utility of a consumer for all combinations goods consumed. Represents both their welfare and their preferences.
Utility	Utility refers to the want-satisfying power of a good or service; the satisfaction or pleasure a consumer obtains from the consumption of a good or service.
Consumption	In Keynesian economics consumption refers to personal consumption expenditure, i.e., the purchase of currently produced goods and services out of income, out of savings (net worth), or from borrowed funds. It refers to that part of disposable income that does not go to saving.
Preference	The act of a debtor in paying or securing one or more of his creditors in a manner more favorable to them than to other creditors or to the exclusion of such other creditors is a preference. In the absence of statute, a preference is perfectly good, but to be legal it must be bona fide, and not a mere subterfuge of the debtor to secure a future benefit to himself or to prevent the application of his property to his debts.
Revealed preference	Revealed preference refers to the use of the value of expenditure to 'reveal' the preference of a consumer or group of consumers for the bundle of goods they purchase compared to other bundles of equal or smaller value.
Argument	The discussion by counsel for the respective parties of their contentions on the law and the facts of the case being tried in order to aid the jury in arriving at a correct and just conclusion is called argument.
Yield	The interest rate that equates a future value or an annuity to a given present value is a yield.
Demand curve	Demand curve refers to the graph of quantity demanded as a function of price, normally downward sloping, straight or curved, and drawn with quantity on the horizontal axis and price on the vertical axis.
Operation	A standardized method or technique that is performed repetitively, often on different materials resulting in different finished goods is called an operation.
Gains from trade	The net increase in output that countries experience as a result of lowering import tariffs and otherwise liberalizing trade is referred to as gains from trade.
Gain	In finance, gain is a profit or an increase in value of an investment such as a stock or bond. Gain is calculated by fair market value or the proceeds from the sale of the investment minus the sum of the purchase price and all costs associated with it.
Income effect	Income effect refers to that portion of the effect of price on quantity demanded that reflects the change in real income due to the price change.
Policy	Similar to a script in that a policy can be a less than completely rational decision-making method. Involves the use of a pre-existing set of decision steps for any problem that presents itself.
Equivalent variation	Equivalent variation refers to the amount of money that, paid to a person, group, or whole economy, would make them as well off as a specified change in the economy.
Welfare	Welfare refers to the economic well being of an individual, group, or economy. For individuals, it is conceptualized by a utility function. For groups, including countries and the world, it is a tricky philosophical concept, since individuals fare differently.
Slope	The slope of a line in the plane containing the x and y axes is generally represented by the letter m, and is defined as the change in the y coordinate divided by the corresponding change in the x coordinate, between two distinct points on the line.
Compensating	Compensating variation refers to an amount of money that just compensates a person, group, or

variation	whole economy, for the welfare effects of a change in the economy, thus providing a monetary measure of that change in welfare.
Indifference curve	Indifference curve refers to a means of representing the preferences and well being of consumers. Formally, it is a curve representing the combinations of arguments in a utility function that yield a given level of utility.
Budget line	Given an allocation of two goods, the budget line through that allocation is the set of all other allocations of the two goods that someone in a market could arrive at by selling one of the goods for the other.
Budget	Budget refers to an account, usually for a year, of the planned expenditures and the expected receipts of an entity. For a government, the receipts are tax revenues.
Supply curve	Supply curve refers to the graph of quantity supplied as a function of price, normally upward sloping, straight or curved, and drawn with quantity on the horizontal axis and price on the vertical axis.
Supply	Supply is the aggregate amount of any material good that can be called into being at a certain price point; it comprises one half of the equation of supply and demand. In classical economic theory, a curve representing supply is one of the factors that produce price.
Analogy	Analogy is either the cognitive process of transferring information from a particular subject to another particular subject (the target), or a linguistic expression corresponding to such a process. In a narrower sense, analogy is an inference or an argument from a particular to another particular, as opposed to deduction, induction, and abduction, where at least one of the premises or the conclusion is general.
Firm	An organization that employs resources to produce a good or service for profit and owns and operates one or more plants is referred to as a firm.
Market price	Market price is an economic concept with commonplace familiarity; it is the price that a good or service is offered at, or will fetch, in the marketplace; it is of interest mainly in the study of microeconomics.
Market	A market is, as defined in economics, a social arrangement that allows buyers and sellers to discover information and carry out a voluntary exchange of goods or services.
Profit	Profit refers to the return to the resource entrepreneurial ability; total revenue minus total cost.
Consumer surplus	The difference between the maximum that consumers would be willing to pay for a good and what they actually do pay is consumer surplus. For each unit of the good, this is the vertical distance between the demand curve and price.
Economic policy	Economic policy refers to the actions that governments take in the economic field. It covers the systems for setting interest rates and government deficit as well as the labor market, national ownership, and many other areas of government.
Competitive market	A market in which no buyer or seller has market power is called a competitive market.
Producer surplus	The difference between the revenue of producers and production cost, measured as the area above the supply curve and below price, out to the quantity supplied, and net of fixed cost and losses at low output is producer surplus. If input prices are constant, this is profit.
Price ceiling	Price ceiling refers to a government-imposed upper limit on the price that may be charged for a product. If that limit is binding, it implies a situation of excess demand and shortage.
Coupon	In finance, a coupon is "attached" to a bond, either physically (as with old bonds) or electronically. Each coupon represents a predetermined payment promized to the bond-holder in

Go to **Cram101.com** for the Practice Tests for this Chapter.

Go to **Cram101.com** for the Practice Tests for this Chapter.
And, **NEVER** highlight a book again!

	return for his or her loan of money to the bond-issuer. .
Average cost	Average cost is equal to total cost divided by the number of goods produced (Quantity-Q). It is also equal to the sum of average variable costs (total variable costs divided by Q) plus average fixed costs (total fixed costs divided by Q).
Distribution	Distribution in economics, the manner in which total output and income is distributed among individuals or factors.
Household	An economic unit that provides the economy with resources and uses the income received to purchase goods and services that satisfy economic wants is called household.
Tax reform	Tax reform is the process of changing the way taxes are collected or managed by the government. Some seek to reduce the level of taxation of all people by the government. Some seek to make the tax system more/less progressive in its effect. Some may be trying to make the tax system more understandable, or more accountable.
Economics	The social science dealing with the use of scarce resources to obtain the maximum satisfaction of society's virtually unlimited economic wants is an economics.
Journal	Book of original entry, in which transactions are recorded in a general ledger system, is referred to as a journal.
Service	Service refers to a "non tangible product" that is not embodied in a physical good and that typically effects some change in another product, person, or institution. Contrasts with good.
Revenue	Revenue is a U.S. business term for the amount of money that a company receives from its activities, mostly from sales of products and/or services to customers.
Industry	A group of firms that produce identical or similar products is an industry. It is also used specifically to refer to an area of economic production focused on manufacturing which involves large amounts of capital investment before any profit can be realized, also called "heavy industry".
Budget constraint	Budget constraint refers to the maximum quantity of goods that could be purchased for a given level of income and a given set of prices.
Integration	Economic integration refers to reducing barriers among countries to transactions and to movements of goods, capital, and labor, including harmonization of laws, regulations, and standards. Integrated markets theoretically function as a unified market.

Market	A market is, as defined in economics, a social arrangement that allows buyers and sellers to discover information and carry out a voluntary exchange of goods or services.
Demand curve	Demand curve refers to the graph of quantity demanded as a function of price, normally downward sloping, straight or curved, and drawn with quantity on the horizontal axis and price on the vertical axis.
Property	Assets defined in the broadest legal sense. Property includes the unrealized receivables of a cash basis taxpayer, but not services rendered.
Revenue	Revenue is a U.S. business term for the amount of money that a company receives from its activities, mostly from sales of products and/or services to customers.
Aggregate demand	The total demand for a country's output, including demands for consumption, investment, government purchases, and net exports is referred to as aggregate demand.
Aggregate demand function	The relationship between aggregate output and aggregate demand that shows the quantity of aggregate output demanded at each level of aggregate output is called aggregate demand function.
Holding	The holding is a court's determination of a matter of law based on the issue presented in the particular case. In other words: under this law, with these facts, this result.
Economy	The income, expenditures, and resources that affect the cost of running a business and household are called an economy.
Aggregate demand curve	Aggregate demand curve refers to the quantities of total output economic agents are prepared to demand at different price levels.
Complement	A good that is used in conjunction with another good is a complement. For example, cameras and film would complement eachother.
Normal good	A good or service whose consumption increases when income increases and falls when income decreases when price remains constant is referred to as normal good.
Market price	Market price is an economic concept with commonplace familiarity; it is the price that a good or service is offered at, or will fetch, in the marketplace; it is of interest mainly in the study of microeconomics.
Marginal rate of substitution	In economics, the marginal rate of substitution is the rate at which consumers are willing to give up units of one good in exchange for more units of another good.
Operation	A standardized method or technique that is performed repetitively, often on different materials resulting in different finished goods is called an operation.
Margin	A deposit by a buyer in stocks with a seller or a stockbroker, as security to cover fluctuations in the market in reference to stocks that the buyer has purchased but for which he has not paid is a margin. Commodities are also traded on margin.
Slope	The slope of a line in the plane containing the x and y axes is generally represented by the letter m, and is defined as the change in the y coordinate divided by the corresponding change in the x coordinate, between two distinct points on the line.
Agent	A person who makes economic decisions for another economic actor. A hired manager operates as an agent for a firm's owner.
Quantity demanded	The amount of a good or service that buyers desire to purchase at a particular price during some period is a quantity demanded.
Preference	The act of a debtor in paying or securing one or more of his creditors in a manner more favorable to them than to other creditors or to the exclusion of such other creditors is a preference. In the absence of statute, a preference is perfectly good, but to be legal it

	must be bona fide, and not a mere subterfuge of the debtor to secure a future benefit to himself or to prevent the application of his property to his debts.
Elasticity	In economics, elasticity is the ratio of the incremental percentage change in one variable with respect to an incremental percentage change in another variable. Elasticity is usually expressed as a positive number (i.e., an absolute value) when the sign is already clear from context.
Interest	In finance and economics, interest is the price paid by a borrower for the use of a lender's money. In other words, interest is the amount of paid to "rent" money for a period of time.
Price elasticity	The responsiveness of the market to change in price is called price elasticity. If price elasticity is low, a large change in price will lead to a small change in supply.
Price elasticity of demand	Price elasticity of demand refers to the ratio of the percentage change in quantity demanded of a product or resource to the percentage change in its price; a measure of the responsiveness of buyers to a change in the price of a product or resource.
Derivative	A derivative is a generic term for specific types of investments from which payoffs over time are derived from the performance of assets (such as commodities, shares or bonds), interest rates, exchange rates, or indices (such as a stock market index, consumer price index (CPI) or an index of weather conditions).
Elastic demand	Elastic demand refers to product or resource demand whose price elasticity is greater than 1. This means the resulting change in quantity demanded is greater than the percentage change in price.
Inelastic demand	Inelastic demand refers to product or resource demand for which the elasticity coefficient for price is less than 1. This means the resulting percentage change in quantity demanded is less than the percentage change in price. In other words, consumers are relatively less sensitive to changes in price.
Inelastic	Inelastic refers to having an elasticity less than one. For a price elasticity of demand, this means that expenditure falls as price falls. For an income elasticity, it means that expenditure share falls with income.
Perfect substitute	A good that is regarded by its demanders as identical to another good, so that the elasticity of substitution between them is infinite is referred to as perfect substitute.
Strike	The withholding of labor services by an organized group of workers is referred to as a strike.
Profit	Profit refers to the return to the resource entrepreneurial ability; total revenue minus total cost.
Production	The creation of finished goods and services using the factors of production: land, labor, capital, entrepreneurship, and knowledge.
Supply	Supply is the aggregate amount of any material good that can be called into being at a certain price point; it comprises one half of the equation of supply and demand. In classical economic theory, a curve representing supply is one of the factors that produce price.
Marginal revenue	Marginal revenue refers to the change in total revenue obtained by selling one additional unit.
Unit elastic	Unit elastic refers to having an elasticity coefficient equal to one. For a price elasticity of demand, this means that revenue remains constant as price changes.
Labor	People's physical and mental talents and efforts that are used to help produce goods and services are called labor.

Go to **Cram101.com** for the Practice Tests for this Chapter.

Marginal revenue curve	A graph of the relationship between the change in total revenue and the quantity sold is referred to as the marginal revenue curve.
Income elasticity	Normally the income elasticity of demand; that is, the elasticity of demand with respect to income. Measured as the percentage change in demand relative to the percentage change in income.
Inferior good	Inferior good refers to a good for which the demand falls as income rises. The income elasticity of demand is therefore negative.
Income elasticity of demand	In economics, the income elasticity of demand measures the responsiveness of the quantity demanded of a good to the income of the people demanding the good.
Budget constraint	Budget constraint refers to the maximum quantity of goods that could be purchased for a given level of income and a given set of prices.
Budget	Budget refers to an account, usually for a year, of the planned expenditures and the expected receipts of an entity. For a government, the receipts are tax revenues.
Purchasing	Purchasing refers to the function in a firm that searches for quality material resources, finds the best suppliers, and negotiates the best price for goods and services.
Unitary elasticity	A demand relationship in which the percentage change in quantity of a product demanded is the same as the percentage change in price in absolute value is called unitary elasticity.
Laffer curve	A curve relating government tax rates and tax revenues and on which a particular tax rate maximizes tax revenues is a Laffer curve.
Labor market	Any arrangement that brings buyers and sellers of labor services together to agree on conditions of work and pay is called a labor market.
Wage	The payment for the service of a unit of labor, per unit time. In trade theory, it is the only payment to labor, usually unskilled labor. In empirical work, wage data may exclude other compenzation, which must be added to get the total cost of employment.
Firm	An organization that employs resources to produce a good or service for profit and owns and operates one or more plants is referred to as a firm.
Supply of labor	Supply of labor refers to the relationship between the quantity of labor supplied by employees and the real wage rate when all other influences on work plans remain the same.
Labor supply	The number of workers available to an economy. The principal determinants of labor supply are population, real wages, and social traditions.
Yield	The interest rate that equates a future value or an annuity to a given present value is a yield.
Elasticity of labor supply	The percentage change in the quantity of labor supplied divided by the percentage change in wage rate is an elasticity of labor supply.

Demand curve	Demand curve refers to the graph of quantity demanded as a function of price, normally downward sloping, straight or curved, and drawn with quantity on the horizontal axis and price on the vertical axis.
Market	A market is, as defined in economics, a social arrangement that allows buyers and sellers to discover information and carry out a voluntary exchange of goods or services.
Supply curve	Supply curve refers to the graph of quantity supplied as a function of price, normally upward sloping, straight or curved, and drawn with quantity on the horizontal axis and price on the vertical axis.
Supply	Supply is the aggregate amount of any material good that can be called into being at a certain price point; it comprises one half of the equation of supply and demand. In classical economic theory, a curve representing supply is one of the factors that produce price.
Labor	People's physical and mental talents and efforts that are used to help produce goods and services are called labor.
Market price	Market price is an economic concept with commonplace familiarity; it is the price that a good or service is offered at, or will fetch, in the marketplace; it is of interest mainly in the study of microeconomics.
Competitive market	A market in which no buyer or seller has market power is called a competitive market.
Agent	A person who makes economic decisions for another economic actor. A hired manager operates as an agent for a firm's owner.
Equilibrium price	Equilibrium price refers to the price in a competitive market at which the quantity demanded and the quantity supplied are equal, there is neither a shortage nor a surplus, and there is no tendency for price to rise or fall.
Economic equilibrium	Economic equilibrium often refers to an equilibrium in a market that "clears": this is the case where a market for a product has attained the price where the amount supplied of a certain product equals the quantity demanded.
Industry	A group of firms that produce identical or similar products is an industry. It is also used specifically to refer to an area of economic production focused on manufacturing which involves large amounts of capital investment before any profit can be realized, also called "heavy industry".
Equilibrium quantity	Equilibrium quantity refers to the quantity demanded and supplied at the equilibrium price in a competitive market; the profit-maximizing output of a firm.
Slope	The slope of a line in the plane containing the x and y axes is generally represented by the letter m, and is defined as the change in the y coordinate divided by the corresponding change in the x coordinate, between two distinct points on the line.
Comparative static	The comparison of two equilibria from a static model, usually differing by the effects of a single small change in an exogenous variable is a comparative static.
Demand price	Demand price refers to the price at which a given quantity is demanded; the demand curve viewed from the perspective of price as a function of quantity.
Supply price	Supply price refers to the price at which a given quantity is supplied; the supply curve viewed from the perspective of price as a function of quantity.
Comparative statics	Comparative statics is the comparison of two different equilibrium states, before and after a change in one of the variables. Being a study of statics it compares two different unchanging points, once they have changed. It does not study the motion towards equilibrium, nor the process of the change itself.

Go to **Cram101.com** for the Practice Tests for this Chapter.

Economic policy	Economic policy refers to the actions that governments take in the economic field. It covers the systems for setting interest rates and government deficit as well as the labor market, national ownership, and many other areas of government.
Interest	In finance and economics, interest is the price paid by a borrower for the use of a lender's money. In other words, interest is the amount of paid to "rent" money for a period of time.
Policy	Similar to a script in that a policy can be a less than completely rational decision-making method. Involves the use of a pre-existing set of decision steps for any problem that presents itself.
Sales tax	A sales tax is a tax on consumption. It is normally a certain percentage that is added onto the price of a good or service that is purchased.
Bid	A bid price is a price offered by a buyer when he/she buys a good. In the context of stock trading on a stock exchange, the bid price is the highest price a buyer of a stock is willing to pay for a share of that given stock.
Profit	Profit refers to the return to the resource entrepreneurial ability; total revenue minus total cost.
Firm	An organization that employs resources to produce a good or service for profit and owns and operates one or more plants is referred to as a firm.
Elastic supply	Elastic supply refers to product or resource supply whose price elasticity is greater than 1. This means the resulting change in quantity supplied is greater than the percentage change in price.
Inelastic supply	Inelastic supply refers to product or resource supply for which the price elasticity coefficient is less than 1. The percentage change in quantity supplied is less than the percentage change in price.
Inelastic	Inelastic refers to having an elasticity less than one. For a price elasticity of demand, this means that expenditure falls as price falls. For an income elasticity, it means that expenditure share falls with income.
Perfectly inelastic supply	Perfectly inelastic supply refers to product or resource supply in which price can be of any amount at a particular quantity of the product or resource demanded; quantity supplied does not respond to a change in price; graphs as a vertical supply curve.
Deadweight loss	Deadweight loss refers to the net loss in economic welfare that is caused by a tariff or tax, defined as the total losses to those who lose, minus the total gains to those who gain.
Social cost	Social cost, in economics, is the total of all the costs associated with an economic activity. It includes both costs borne by the economic agent and also all costs borne by society at large. It includes the costs reflected in the organization's production function and the costs external to the firm's private costs.
Revenue	Revenue is a U.S. business term for the amount of money that a company receives from its activities, mostly from sales of products and/or services to customers.
Gain	In finance, gain is a profit or an increase in value of an investment such as a stock or bond. Gain is calculated by fair market value or the proceeds from the sale of the investment minus the sum of the purchase price and all costs associated with it.
Interest rate	The rate of return on bonds, loans, or deposits. When one speaks of 'the' interest rate, it is usually in a model where there is only one.
Economy	The income, expenditures, and resources that affect the cost of running a business and household are called an economy.

Lender	Suppliers and financial institutions that lend money to companies is referred to as a lender.
Interest payment	The payment to holders of bonds payable, calculated by multiplying the stated rate on the face of the bond by the par, or face, value of the bond. If bonds are issued at a discount or premium, the interest payment does not equal the interest expense.
Interest income	Interest income refers to payments of income to those who supply the economy with capital.
Deductible	The dollar sum of costs that an insured individual must pay before the insurer begins to pay is called deductible.
Subsidy	Subsidy refers to government financial assistance to a domestic producer.
Remainder	A remainder in property law is a future interest created in a transferee that is capable of becoming possessory upon the natural termination of a prior estate created by the same instrument.
Total supply	Total supply refers to the supply schedule or the supply curve of all sellers of a good or service.
Total demand	Total demand refers to the demand schedule or the demand curve of all buyers of a good or service; also called market demand.
Pareto efficiency	A condition in which no change is possible that will make some members of society better off without making some other members of society worse off is referred to as pareto efficiency. It is a central concept in economics with broad applications in game theory, engineering and the social sciences.
Willingness to pay	Willingness to pay refers to the largest amount of money that an individual or group could pay, along with a change in policy, without being made worse off.
Marginal rate of substitution	In economics, the marginal rate of substitution is the rate at which consumers are willing to give up units of one good in exchange for more units of another good.
Allocate	Allocate refers to the assignment of income for various tax purposes. A multistate corporation's nonbusiness income usually is distributed to the state where the nonbusiness assets are located; it is not apportioned with the rest of the entity's income.
Gains from trade	The net increase in output that countries experience as a result of lowering import tariffs and otherwise liberalizing trade is referred to as gains from trade.
Buyer	A buyer refers to a role in the buying center with formal authority and responsibility to select the supplier and negotiate the terms of the contract.
Net loss	Net loss refers to the amount by which expenses exceed revenues. The difference between income received and expenses, when expenses are greater.
Single market	A single market is a customs union with common policies on product regulation, and freedom of movement of all the four factors of production (goods, services, capital and labor).

Auction	A preexisting business model that operates successfully on the Internet by announcing an item for sale and permitting multiple purchasers to bid on them under specified rules and condition is an auction.
Cartel	Cartel refers to a group of firms that seeks to raise the price of a good by restricting its supply. The term is usually used for international groups, especially involving state-owned firms and/or governments.
Consultant	A professional that provides expert advice in a particular field or area in which customers occassionaly require this type of knowledge is a consultant.
Firm	An organization that employs resources to produce a good or service for profit and owns and operates one or more plants is referred to as a firm.
Federal Communications Commission	Federal Communications Commission refers to the federal authority empowered to license radio and TV stations and to assign wavelengths to stations 'in the public interest'.
Service	Service refers to a "non tangible product" that is not embodied in a physical good and that typically effects some change in another product, person, or institution. Contrasts with good.
Market value	Market value refers to the price of an asset agreed on between a willing buyer and a willing seller; the price an asset could demand if it is sold on the open market.
Market	A market is, as defined in economics, a social arrangement that allows buyers and sellers to discover information and carry out a voluntary exchange of goods or services.
Bid	A bid price is a price offered by a buyer when he/she buys a good. In the context of stock trading on a stock exchange, the bid price is the highest price a buyer of a stock is willing to pay for a share of that given stock.
Pareto efficiency	A condition in which no change is possible that will make some members of society better off without making some other members of society worse off is referred to as pareto efficiency. It is a central concept in economics with broad applications in game theory, engineering and the social sciences.
Profit	Profit refers to the return to the resource entrepreneurial ability; total revenue minus total cost.
Yield	The interest rate that equates a future value or an annuity to a given present value is a yield.
Profit maximization	Search by a firm for the product quantity, quality, and price that gives that firm the highest possible profit is profit maximization.
Distribution	Distribution in economics, the manner in which total output and income is distributed among individuals or factors.
Buyer	A buyer refers to a role in the buying center with formal authority and responsibility to select the supplier and negotiate the terms of the contract.
Valuation	In finance, valuation is the process of estimating the market value of a financial asset or liability. They can be done on assets (for example, investments in marketable securities such as stocks, options, business enterprises, or intangible assets such as patents and trademarks) or on liabilities (e.g., Bonds issued by a company).
Agent	A person who makes economic decisions for another economic actor. A hired manager operates as an agent for a firm's owner.
Interest	In finance and economics, interest is the price paid by a borrower for the use of a lender's

	money. In other words, interest is the amount of paid to "rent" money for a period of time.
Users	Users refer to people in the organization who actually use the product or service purchased by the buying center.
EBay	eBay manages an online auction and shopping website, where people buy and sell goods and services worldwide.
Property	Assets defined in the broadest legal sense. Property includes the unrealized receivables of a cash basis taxpayer, but not services rendered.
License	A license in the sphere of Intellectual Property Rights (IPR) is a document, contract or agreement giving permission or the 'right' to a legally-definable entity to do something (such as manufacture a product or to use a service), or to apply something (such as a trademark), with the objective of achieving commercial gain.
Journal	Book of original entry, in which transactions are recorded in a general ledger system, is referred to as a journal.
Economic perspective	A viewpoint that envisions individuals and institutions making rational decisions by comparing the marginal benefits and marginal costs associated with their actions is an economic perspective.
Strategic choice	Strategic choice refers to an organization's strategy; the ways an organization will attempt to fulfill its mission and achieve its long-term goals.
Collusion	Collusion refers to cooperation among firms to raise price and otherwise increase their profits.

Firm	An organization that employs resources to produce a good or service for profit and owns and operates one or more plants is referred to as a firm.
Inputs	The inputs used by a firm or an economy are the labor, raw materials, electricity and other resources it uses to produce its outputs.
Consumer theory	Consumer theory is a theory of economics. It relates preferences, indifference curves and budget constraints to consumer demand curves. The mathematical models that make up consumer theory can be used in a constrained optimization problem to estimate the optimal goods bundle for an individual buyer.
Production	The creation of finished goods and services using the factors of production: land, labor, capital, entrepreneurship, and knowledge.
Factors of production	Economic resources: land, capital, labor, and entrepreneurial ability are called factors of production.
Technology	The body of knowledge and techniques that can be used to combine economic resources to produce goods and services is called technology.
Capital	Capital generally refers to financial wealth, especially that used to start or maintain a business. In classical economics, capital is one of four factors of production, the others being land and labor and entrepreneurship.
Labor	People's physical and mental talents and efforts that are used to help produce goods and services are called labor.
Raw material	Raw material refers to a good that has not been transformed by production; a primary product.
Isoquant	A curve representing the combinations of factor inputs that yield a given level of output in a production function is referred to as isoquant.
Utility	Utility refers to the want-satisfying power of a good or service; the satisfaction or pleasure a consumer obtains from the consumption of a good or service.
Complement	A good that is used in conjunction with another good is a complement. For example, cameras and film would complement eachother.
Perfect complements	Two goods with right-angle indifference curves are perfect complements. Complements are products consumed simultaneously.
Perfect substitute	A good that is regarded by its demanders as identical to another good, so that the elasticity of substitution between them is infinite is referred to as perfect substitute.
Production function	Production function refers to a function that specifies the output in an industry for all combinations of inputs.
Utility function	Utility function refers to a function that specifies the utility of a consumer for all combinations goods consumed. Represents both their welfare and their preferences.
Property	Assets defined in the broadest legal sense. Property includes the unrealized receivables of a cash basis taxpayer, but not services rendered.
Indifference curve	Indifference curve refers to a means of representing the preferences and well being of consumers. Formally, it is a curve representing the combinations of arguments in a utility function that yield a given level of utility.
Argument	The discussion by counsel for the respective parties of their contentions on the law and the facts of the case being tried in order to aid the jury in arriving at a correct and just conclusion is called argument.
Weighted average	The weighted average unit cost of the goods available for sale for both cost of goods sold

Go to **Cram101.com** for the Practice Tests for this Chapter.

101

103

	and ending inventory.
Marginal product	In a production function, the marginal product of a factor is the increase in output due to a unit increase in the input of the factor; that is, the partial derivative of the production function with respect to the factor.
Slope	The slope of a line in the plane containing the x and y axes is generally represented by the letter m, and is defined as the change in the y coordinate divided by the corresponding change in the x coordinate, between two distinct points on the line.
Diminishing marginal product	The property whereby the marginal product of an input declines as the quantity of the input increases is a diminishing marginal product.
Holding	The holding is a court's determination of a matter of law based on the issue presented in the particular case. In other words: under this law, with these facts, this result.
Returns to scale	Returns to scale refers to a technical property of production that predicts what happens to output if the quantity of all input factors is increased by some amount of scale.
Short run	Short run refers to a period of time that permits an increase or decrease in current production volume with existing capacity, but one that is too short to permit enlargement of that capacity itself (eg, the building of new plants, training of additional workers, etc.).
Long run	In economic models, the long run time frame assumes no fixed factors of production. Firms can enter or leave the marketplace, and the cost (and availability) of land, labor, raw materials, and capital goods can be assumed to vary.
Factor of production	Factor of production refers to economic resources used in production such as land, labor, and capital.
Diminishing returns	The fall in the marginal product of a factor or factors that eventually occurs as input of that factor rises, holding the input of at least one other factor fixed, according to the Law of Diminishing Returns.
Preference	The act of a debtor in paying or securing one or more of his creditors in a manner more favorable to them than to other creditors or to the exclusion of such other creditors is a preference. In the absence of statute, a preference is perfectly good, but to be legal it must be bona fide, and not a mere subterfuge of the debtor to secure a future benefit to himself or to prevent the application of his property to his debts.
Variable	A variable is something measured by a number; it is used to analyze what happens to other things when the size of that number changes.
Constant returns to scale	Constant returns to scale refers to a property of a production function such that scaling all inputs by any positive constant also scales output by the same constant. Such a function is also called homogeneous of degree one or linearly homogeneous.
Increasing returns	An increase in a firm's output by a larger percentage than the percentage increase in its inputs is increasing returns.
Decreasing returns to scale	Decreasing returns to scale refers to a property of a production function such that changing all inputs by the same proportion changes output less than in proportion. Example: a function homogeneous of degree less than one.
Supply	Supply is the aggregate amount of any material good that can be called into being at a certain price point; it comprises one half of the equation of supply and demand. In classical economic theory, a curve representing supply is one of the factors that produce price.

Production	The creation of finished goods and services using the factors of production: land, labor, capital, entrepreneurship, and knowledge.
Profit	Profit refers to the return to the resource entrepreneurial ability; total revenue minus total cost.
Firm	An organization that employs resources to produce a good or service for profit and owns and operates one or more plants is referred to as a firm.
Profit maximization	Search by a firm for the product quantity, quality, and price that gives that firm the highest possible profit is profit maximization.
Revenue	Revenue is a U.S. business term for the amount of money that a company receives from its activities, mostly from sales of products and/or services to customers.
Market price	Market price is an economic concept with commonplace familiarity; it is the price that a good or service is offered at, or will fetch, in the marketplace; it is of interest mainly in the study of microeconomics.
Market	A market is, as defined in economics, a social arrangement that allows buyers and sellers to discover information and carry out a voluntary exchange of goods or services.
Factors of production	Economic resources: land, capital, labor, and entrepreneurial ability are called factors of production.
Open market	In economics, the open market is the term used to refer to the environment in which bonds are bought and sold.
Labor	People's physical and mental talents and efforts that are used to help produce goods and services are called labor.
Wage	The payment for the service of a unit of labor, per unit time. In trade theory, it is the only payment to labor, usually unskilled labor. In empirical work, wage data may exclude other compenzation, which must be added to get the total cost of employment.
Opportunity cost	The cost of something in terms of opportunity foregone. The opportunity cost to a country of producing a unit more of a good, such as for export or to replace an import, is the quantity of some other good that could have been produced instead.
Inputs	The inputs used by a firm or an economy are the labor, raw materials, electricity and other resources it uses to produce its outputs.
Historical cost	In accounting terminology, historical cost describes the original cost of an asset at the time of purchase or payment as opposed to its market value
Economic profit	In Economics, a firm is said to be making an economic profit when its revenue exceeds the total opportunity cost of its inputs. It is said to be making an accounting profit if its revenues exceed the total price the firm pays for those inputs. This is sometimes referred to as producer's surplus.
Economic cost	Economic cost refers to payments made or incomes forgone to obtain and retain the services of a resource.
Capital	Capital generally refers to financial wealth, especially that used to start or maintain a business. In classical economics, capital is one of four factors of production, the others being land and labor and entrepreneurship.
Stock market	An organized marketplace in which common stocks are traded. In the United States, the largest stock market is the New York Stock Exchange, on which are traded the stocks of the largest U.S. companies.
Market value	Market value refers to the price of an asset agreed on between a willing buyer and a willing

	seller; the price an asset could demand if it is sold on the open market.
Economy	The income, expenditures, and resources that affect the cost of running a business and household are called an economy.
Stock	In financial terminology, stock is the capital raized by a corporation, through the issuance and sale of shares.
Legal entity	A legal entity is a legal construct through which the law allows a group of natural persons to act as if it were an individual for certain purposes. The most common purposes are lawsuits, property ownership, and contracts.
Corporation	A legal entity chartered by a state or the Federal government that is distinct and separate from the individuals who own it is a corporation. This separation gives the corporation unique powers which other legal entities lack.
Partnership	In the common law, a partnership is a type of business entity in which partners share with each other the profits or losses of the business undertaking in which they have all invested.
Operation	A standardized method or technique that is performed repetitively, often on different materials resulting in different finished goods is called an operation.
Service	Service refers to a "non tangible product" that is not embodied in a physical good and that typically effects some change in another product, person, or institution. Contrasts with good.
Financial market	In economics, a financial market is a mechanism which allows people to trade money for securities or commodities such as gold or other precious metals. In general, any commodity market might be considered to be a financial market, if the usual purpose of traders is not the immediate consumption of the commodity, but rather as a means of delaying or accelerating consumption over time.
Interest rate	The rate of return on bonds, loans, or deposits. When one speaks of 'the' interest rate, it is usually in a model where there is only one.
Consumption	In Keynesian economics consumption refers to personal consumption expenditure, i.e., the purchase of currently produced goods and services out of income, out of savings (net worth), or from borrowed funds. It refers to that part of disposable income that does not go to saving.
Interest	In finance and economics, interest is the price paid by a borrower for the use of a lender's money. In other words, interest is the amount of paid to "rent" money for a period of time.
Investment	Investment refers to spending for the production and accumulation of capital and additions to inventories. In a financial sense, buying an asset with the expectation of making a return.
Stock certificate	Evidence of stock ownership that specifies the name of the company, the number of shares it represents, and the type of stock being issued is referred to as the stock certificate.
Shares	Shares refer to an equity security, representing a shareholder's ownership of a corporation. Shares are one of a finite number of equal portions in the capital of a company, entitling the owner to a proportion of distributed, non-reinvested profits known as dividends and to a portion of the value of the company in case of liquidation.
Dividend	Amount of corporate profits paid out for each share of stock is referred to as dividend.
A share	In finance the term A share has two distinct meanings, both relating to securities. The first is a designation for a 'class' of common or preferred stock. A share of common or preferred stock typically has enhanced voting rights or other benefits compared to the other forms of shares that may have been created. The equity structure, or how many types of shares are offered, is determined by the corporate charter.

Go to **Cram101.com** for the Practice Tests for this Chapter.
And, **NEVER** highlight a book again!

Present value	The value today of a stream of payments and/or receipts over time in the future and/or the past, converted to the present using an interest rate. If X t is the amount in period t and r the interest rate, then present value at time t=0 is V = ?T /t.
Shareholder	A shareholder is an individual or company (including a corporation) that legally owns one or more shares of stock in a joined stock company.
Budget set	A budget set includes all possible consumption bundles that someone can afford given the prices of goods and the person's income level. The budget set is bounded above by the budget line.
Budget	Budget refers to an account, usually for a year, of the planned expenditures and the expected receipts of an entity. For a government, the receipts are tax revenues.
Variable	A variable is something measured by a number; it is used to analyze what happens to other things when the size of that number changes.
Long run	In economic models, the long run time frame assumes no fixed factors of production. Firms can enter or leave the marketplace, and the cost (and availability) of land, labor, raw materials, and capital goods can be assumed to vary.
Short run	Short run refers to a period of time that permits an increase or decrease in current production volume with existing capacity, but one that is too short to permit enlargement of that capacity itself (eg, the building of new plants, training of additional workers, etc.).
Lease	A contract for the possession and use of land or other property, including goods, on one side, and a recompense of rent or other income on the other is the lease.
Marginal product	In a production function, the marginal product of a factor is the increase in output due to a unit increase in the input of the factor; that is, the partial derivative of the production function with respect to the factor.
Value of the marginal product	The marginal product of an input times the price of the output is a value of the marginal product.
Factor price	Factor price refers to the price paid for the services of a unit of a primary factor of production per unit time. Includes the wage or salary of labor and the rental prices of land and capital, and normal profits for the entrepreneur.
Fixed cost	The cost that a firm bears if it does not produce at all and that is independent of its output. The presence of a fixed cost tends to imply increasing returns to scale. Contrasts with variable cost.
Slope	The slope of a line in the plane containing the x and y axes is generally represented by the letter m, and is defined as the change in the y coordinate divided by the corresponding change in the x coordinate, between two distinct points on the line.
Production function	Production function refers to a function that specifies the output in an industry for all combinations of inputs.
Comparative static	The comparison of two equilibria from a static model, usually differing by the effects of a single small change in an exogenous variable is a comparative static.
Comparative statics	Comparative statics is the comparison of two different equilibrium states, before and after a change in one of the variables. Being a study of statics it compares two different unchanging points, once they have changed. It does not study the motion towards equilibrium, nor the process of the change itself.
Supply	Supply is the aggregate amount of any material good that can be called into being at a certain price point; it comprises one half of the equation of supply and demand. In classical

economic theory, a curve representing supply is one of the factors that produce price.

Demand curve	Demand curve refers to the graph of quantity demanded as a function of price, normally downward sloping, straight or curved, and drawn with quantity on the horizontal axis and price on the vertical axis.
Argument	The discussion by counsel for the respective parties of their contentions on the law and the facts of the case being tried in order to aid the jury in arriving at a correct and just conclusion is called argument.
Diminishing marginal product	The property whereby the marginal product of an input declines as the quantity of the input increases is a diminishing marginal product.
Returns to scale	Returns to scale refers to a technical property of production that predicts what happens to output if the quantity of all input factors is increased by some amount of scale.
Constant returns to scale	Constant returns to scale refers to a property of a production function such that scaling all inputs by any positive constant also scales output by the same constant. Such a function is also called homogeneous of degree one or linearly homogeneous.
Decreasing returns to scale	Decreasing returns to scale refers to a property of a production function such that changing all inputs by the same proportion changes output less than in proportion. Example: a function homogeneous of degree less than one.
Competitor	Other organizations in the same industry or type of business that provide a good or service to the same set of customers is referred to as a competitor.
Technology	The body of knowledge and techniques that can be used to combine economic resources to produce goods and services is called technology.
Yield	The interest rate that equates a future value or an annuity to a given present value is a yield.
Competitive firm	Competitive firm refers to a firm without market power, with no ability to alter the market price of the goods it produces.
Supply curve	Supply curve refers to the graph of quantity supplied as a function of price, normally upward sloping, straight or curved, and drawn with quantity on the horizontal axis and price on the vertical axis.
Points	Loan origination fees that may be deductible as interest by a buyer of property. A seller of property who pays points reduces the selling price by the amount of the points paid for the buyer.
Aid	Assistance provided by countries and by international institutions such as the World Bank to developing countries in the form of monetary grants, loans at low interest rates, in kind, or a combination of these is called aid. Aid can also refer to assistance of any type rendered to benefit some group or individual.
Subsidy	Subsidy refers to government financial assistance to a domestic producer.
Standard of living	Standard of living refers to the level of consumption that people enjoy, on the average, and is measured by average income per person.
Total supply	Total supply refers to the supply schedule or the supply curve of all sellers of a good or service.
Factoring	In mathematics, factorization or factoring is the decomposition of an object into a product of other objects, or factors, which when multiplied together give the original.

Profit	Profit refers to the return to the resource entrepreneurial ability; total revenue minus total cost.
Production	The creation of finished goods and services using the factors of production: land, labor, capital, entrepreneurship, and knowledge.
Firm	An organization that employs resources to produce a good or service for profit and owns and operates one or more plants is referred to as a firm.
Production function	Production function refers to a function that specifies the output in an industry for all combinations of inputs.
Cost function	The relationship, expressed as an equation, between a cost and a one or more variables is the cost function. In choosing a cost function both economic plausibility and goodness fit are relevant. It measures how good any particular solution is.
Minimum cost	Minimum cost refers to the lowest attainable cost per unit. Every point on an average cost curve is a minimum in the sense that it is the best the firm can do with respect to cost for the output which that point represents.
Interest	In finance and economics, interest is the price paid by a borrower for the use of a lender's money. In other words, interest is the amount of paid to "rent" money for a period of time.
Isoquant	A curve representing the combinations of factor inputs that yield a given level of output in a production function is referred to as isoquant.
Factor price	Factor price refers to the price paid for the services of a unit of a primary factor of production per unit time. Includes the wage or salary of labor and the rental prices of land and capital, and normal profits for the entrepreneur.
Argument	The discussion by counsel for the respective parties of their contentions on the law and the facts of the case being tried in order to aid the jury in arriving at a correct and just conclusion is called argument.
Budget constraint	Budget constraint refers to the maximum quantity of goods that could be purchased for a given level of income and a given set of prices.
Budget	Budget refers to an account, usually for a year, of the planned expenditures and the expected receipts of an entity. For a government, the receipts are tax revenues.
Inputs	The inputs used by a firm or an economy are the labor, raw materials, electricity and other resources it uses to produce its outputs.
Yield	The interest rate that equates a future value or an annuity to a given present value is a yield.
Conditional factor demands	Conditional factor demands defines the least cost input combination to produce a given level of output. In this sense it is a short run concept since output levels are not free to vary.
Perfect substitute	A good that is regarded by its demanders as identical to another good, so that the elasticity of substitution between them is infinite is referred to as perfect substitute.
Returns to scale	Returns to scale refers to a technical property of production that predicts what happens to output if the quantity of all input factors is increased by some amount of scale.
Technology	The body of knowledge and techniques that can be used to combine economic resources to produce goods and services is called technology.
Constant returns to scale	Constant returns to scale refers to a property of a production function such that scaling all inputs by any positive constant also scales output by the same constant. Such a function is also called homogeneous of degree one or linearly homogeneous.

Variable	A variable is something measured by a number; it is used to analyze what happens to other things when the size of that number changes.
Factors of production	Economic resources: land, capital, labor, and entrepreneurial ability are called factors of production.
Long run	In economic models, the long run time frame assumes no fixed factors of production. Firms can enter or leave the marketplace, and the cost (and availability) of land, labor, raw materials, and capital goods can be assumed to vary.
Short run	Short run refers to a period of time that permits an increase or decrease in current production volume with existing capacity, but one that is too short to permit enlargement of that capacity itself (eg, the building of new plants, training of additional workers, etc.).
Fixed cost	The cost that a firm bears if it does not produce at all and that is independent of its output. The presence of a fixed cost tends to imply increasing returns to scale. Contrasts with variable cost.
Sunk cost	Sunk cost refers to a cost that has been incurred and cannot be recovered to any significant degree.
Interest payment	The payment to holders of bonds payable, calculated by multiplying the stated rate on the face of the bond by the par, or face, value of the bond. If bonds are issued at a discount or premium, the interest payment does not equal the interest expense.
Market	A market is, as defined in economics, a social arrangement that allows buyers and sellers to discover information and carry out a voluntary exchange of goods or services.
Capital	Capital generally refers to financial wealth, especially that used to start or maintain a business. In classical economics, capital is one of four factors of production, the others being land and labor and entrepreneurship.
Increasing returns	An increase in a firm's output by a larger percentage than the percentage increase in its inputs is increasing returns.
Average cost	Average cost is equal to total cost divided by the number of goods produced (Quantity-Q). It is also equal to the sum of average variable costs (total variable costs divided by Q) plus average fixed costs (total fixed costs divided by Q).
Decreasing returns to scale	Decreasing returns to scale refers to a property of a production function such that changing all inputs by the same proportion changes output less than in proportion. Example: a function homogeneous of degree less than one.
Lagrangian	A lagrangian refers to a function constructed in solving economic models that includes minimization and maximization of a function subject to constraints.

Cost curve	A cost curve is a graph of the costs of production as a function of total quantity produced. In a free market economy, productively efficient firms use these curves to find the optimal point of production, where they make the most profits.
Cost function	The relationship, expressed as an equation, between a cost and a one or more variables is the cost function. In choosing a cost function both economic plausibility and goodness fit are relevant. It measures how good any particular solution is.
Firm	An organization that employs resources to produce a good or service for profit and owns and operates one or more plants is referred to as a firm.
Fixed cost	The cost that a firm bears if it does not produce at all and that is independent of its output. The presence of a fixed cost tends to imply increasing returns to scale. Contrasts with variable cost.
Variable cost	The portion of a firm or industry's cost that changes with output, in contrast to fixed cost is referred to as variable cost.
Variable	A variable is something measured by a number; it is used to analyze what happens to other things when the size of that number changes.
Average cost	Average cost is equal to total cost divided by the number of goods produced (Quantity-Q). It is also equal to the sum of average variable costs (total variable costs divided by Q) plus average fixed costs (total fixed costs divided by Q).
Total cost	The sum of fixed cost and variable cost is referred to as total cost.
Average fixed Cost	Average fixed cost refers to total fixed cost divided by the number of units of output; a per-unit measure of fixed costs.
Average variable cost	A firm's total variable cost divided by output is called average variable cost.
Production	The creation of finished goods and services using the factors of production: land, labor, capital, entrepreneurship, and knowledge.
Marginal cost	Marginal cost refers to the increase in cost that accompanies a unit increase in output; the partial derivative of the cost function with respect to output.
Interest	In finance and economics, interest is the price paid by a borrower for the use of a lender's money. In other words, interest is the amount of paid to "rent" money for a period of time.
Argument	The discussion by counsel for the respective parties of their contentions on the law and the facts of the case being tried in order to aid the jury in arriving at a correct and just conclusion is called argument.
Slope	The slope of a line in the plane containing the x and y axes is generally represented by the letter m, and is defined as the change in the y coordinate divided by the corresponding change in the x coordinate, between two distinct points on the line.
Long run	In economic models, the long run time frame assumes no fixed factors of production. Firms can enter or leave the marketplace, and the cost (and availability) of land, labor, raw materials, and capital goods can be assumed to vary.
Short run	Short run refers to a period of time that permits an increase or decrease in current production volume with existing capacity, but one that is too short to permit enlargement of that capacity itself (eg, the building of new plants, training of additional workers, etc.).
Average total cost	Average total cost refers to a firm's total cost divided by output ; equal to average fixed cost plus average variable cost.
Derivative	A derivative is a generic term for specific types of investments from which payoffs over time

are derived from the performance of assets (such as commodities, shares or bonds), interest rates, exchange rates, or indices (such as a stock market index, consumer price index (CPI) or an index of weather conditions).

101

Market	A market is, as defined in economics, a social arrangement that allows buyers and sellers to discover information and carry out a voluntary exchange of goods or services.
Firm	An organization that employs resources to produce a good or service for profit and owns and operates one or more plants is referred to as a firm.
Profit	Profit refers to the return to the resource entrepreneurial ability; total revenue minus total cost.
Inputs	The inputs used by a firm or an economy are the labor, raw materials, electricity and other resources it uses to produce its outputs.
Cost function	The relationship, expressed as an equation, between a cost and a one or more variables is the cost function. In choosing a cost function both economic plausibility and goodness fit are relevant. It measures how good any particular solution is.
Pure competition	A market structure in which a very large number of firms sells a standardized product, into which entry is very easy, in which the individual seller has no control over the product price, and in which there is no non-price competition is pure competition.
Market price	Market price is an economic concept with commonplace familiarity; it is the price that a good or service is offered at, or will fetch, in the marketplace; it is of interest mainly in the study of microeconomics.
Total supply	Total supply refers to the supply schedule or the supply curve of all sellers of a good or service.
Supply	Supply is the aggregate amount of any material good that can be called into being at a certain price point; it comprises one half of the equation of supply and demand. In classical economic theory, a curve representing supply is one of the factors that produce price.
Industry	A group of firms that produce identical or similar products is an industry. It is also used specifically to refer to an area of economic production focused on manufacturing which involves large amounts of capital investment before any profit can be realized, also called "heavy industry".
Competitive firm	Competitive firm refers to a firm without market power, with no ability to alter the market price of the goods it produces.
Demand curve	Demand curve refers to the graph of quantity demanded as a function of price, normally downward sloping, straight or curved, and drawn with quantity on the horizontal axis and price on the vertical axis.
Marginal revenue	Marginal revenue refers to the change in total revenue obtained by selling one additional unit.
Marginal cost	Marginal cost refers to the increase in cost that accompanies a unit increase in output; the partial derivative of the cost function with respect to output.
Revenue	Revenue is a U.S. business term for the amount of money that a company receives from its activities, mostly from sales of products and/or services to customers.
Argument	The discussion by counsel for the respective parties of their contentions on the law and the facts of the case being tried in order to aid the jury in arriving at a correct and just conclusion is called argument.
Supply curve	Supply curve refers to the graph of quantity supplied as a function of price, normally upward sloping, straight or curved, and drawn with quantity on the horizontal axis and price on the vertical axis.
Cost curve	A cost curve is a graph of the costs of production as a function of total quantity produced.

	In a free market economy, productively efficient firms use these curves to find the optimal point of production, where they make the most profits.
Quantity supplied	The amount of a good or service that producers offer to sell at a particular price during a given time period is called quantity supplied.
Points	Loan origination fees that may be deductible as interest by a buyer of property. A seller of property who pays points reduces the selling price by the amount of the points paid for the buyer.
Giffen good	Giffen good refers to a good that is so inferior and so heavily consumed at low incomes that the demand for it rises when its price rises.
Profit maximization	Search by a firm for the product quantity, quality, and price that gives that firm the highest possible profit is profit maximization.
Fixed cost	The cost that a firm bears if it does not produce at all and that is independent of its output. The presence of a fixed cost tends to imply increasing returns to scale. Contrasts with variable cost.
Variable cost	The portion of a firm or industry's cost that changes with output, in contrast to fixed cost is referred to as variable cost.
Variable	A variable is something measured by a number; it is used to analyze what happens to other things when the size of that number changes.
Average variable cost	A firm's total variable cost divided by output is called average variable cost.
Average cost	Average cost is equal to total cost divided by the number of goods produced (Quantity-Q). It is also equal to the sum of average variable costs (total variable costs divided by Q) plus average fixed costs (total fixed costs divided by Q).
Corporation	A legal entity chartered by a state or the Federal government that is distinct and separate from the individuals who own it is a corporation. This separation gives the corporation unique powers which other legal entities lack.
Microsoft	Microsoft is a multinational computer technology corporation with 2004 global annual sales of US$39.79 billion and 71,553 employees in 102 countries and regions as of July 2006. It develops, manufactures, licenses, and supports a wide range of software products for computing devices.
Licensing	Licensing is a form of strategic alliance which involves the sale of a right to use certain proprietary knowledge (so called intellectual property) in a defined way.
Contract	A contract is a "promise" or an "agreement" that is enforced or recognized by the law. In the civil law, a contract is considered to be part of the general law of obligations.
Total cost	The sum of fixed cost and variable cost is referred to as total cost.
Production	The creation of finished goods and services using the factors of production: land, labor, capital, entrepreneurship, and knowledge.
Total revenue	Total revenue refers to the total number of dollars received by a firm from the sale of a product; equal to the total expenditures for the product produced by the firm; equal to the quantity sold multiplied by the price at which it is sold.
Analogy	Analogy is either the cognitive process of transferring information from a particular subject to another particular subject (the target), or a linguistic expression corresponding to such a process. In a narrower sense, analogy is an inference or an argument from a particular to another particular, as opposed to deduction, induction, and abduction, where at least one of

Go to **Cram101.com** for the Practice Tests for this Chapter.

	the premises or the conclusion is general.
Short run	Short run refers to a period of time that permits an increase or decrease in current production volume with existing capacity, but one that is too short to permit enlargement of that capacity itself (eg, the building of new plants, training of additional workers, etc.).
Holding	The holding is a court's determination of a matter of law based on the issue presented in the particular case. In other words: under this law, with these facts, this result.
Long run	In economic models, the long run time frame assumes no fixed factors of production. Firms can enter or leave the marketplace, and the cost (and availability) of land, labor, raw materials, and capital goods can be assumed to vary.
Returns to scale	Returns to scale refers to a technical property of production that predicts what happens to output if the quantity of all input factors is increased by some amount of scale.
Constant returns to scale	Constant returns to scale refers to a property of a production function such that scaling all inputs by any positive constant also scales output by the same constant. Such a function is also called homogeneous of degree one or linearly homogeneous.

Go to **Cram101.com** for the Practice Tests for this Chapter.

Industry	A group of firms that produce identical or similar products is an industry. It is also used specifically to refer to an area of economic production focused on manufacturing which involves large amounts of capital investment before any profit can be realized, also called "heavy industry".
Supply	Supply is the aggregate amount of any material good that can be called into being at a certain price point; it comprises one half of the equation of supply and demand. In classical economic theory, a curve representing supply is one of the factors that produce price.
Firm	An organization that employs resources to produce a good or service for profit and owns and operates one or more plants is referred to as a firm.
Supply curve	Supply curve refers to the graph of quantity supplied as a function of price, normally upward sloping, straight or curved, and drawn with quantity on the horizontal axis and price on the vertical axis.
Individual supply	The supply schedule or supply curve of a single seller is referred to as individual supply.
Demand curve	Demand curve refers to the graph of quantity demanded as a function of price, normally downward sloping, straight or curved, and drawn with quantity on the horizontal axis and price on the vertical axis.
Short run	Short run refers to a period of time that permits an increase or decrease in current production volume with existing capacity, but one that is too short to permit enlargement of that capacity itself (eg, the building of new plants, training of additional workers, etc.).
Market	A market is, as defined in economics, a social arrangement that allows buyers and sellers to discover information and carry out a voluntary exchange of goods or services.
Average cost	Average cost is equal to total cost divided by the number of goods produced (Quantity-Q). It is also equal to the sum of average variable costs (total variable costs divided by Q) plus average fixed costs (total fixed costs divided by Q).
Profit	Profit refers to the return to the resource entrepreneurial ability; total revenue minus total cost.
Long run	In economic models, the long run time frame assumes no fixed factors of production. Firms can enter or leave the marketplace, and the cost (and availability) of land, labor, raw materials, and capital goods can be assumed to vary.
Cost curve	A cost curve is a graph of the costs of production as a function of total quantity produced. In a free market economy, productively efficient firms use these curves to find the optimal point of production, where they make the most profits.
Variable cost	The portion of a firm or industry's cost that changes with output, in contrast to fixed cost is referred to as variable cost.
Variable	A variable is something measured by a number; it is used to analyze what happens to other things when the size of that number changes.
Average variable cost	A firm's total variable cost divided by output is called average variable cost.
Production	The creation of finished goods and services using the factors of production: land, labor, capital, entrepreneurship, and knowledge.
Cost function	The relationship, expressed as an equation, between a cost and a one or more variables is the cost function. In choosing a cost function both economic plausibility and goodness fit are relevant. It measures how good any particular solution is.

Free entry	Free entry refers to the assumption that new firms are permitted to enter an industry without substantial barriers to entry. Together with free exit, it implies that economic profit must be zero in equilibrium.
Points	Loan origination fees that may be deductible as interest by a buyer of property. A seller of property who pays points reduces the selling price by the amount of the points paid for the buyer.
Slope	The slope of a line in the plane containing the x and y axes is generally represented by the letter m, and is defined as the change in the y coordinate divided by the corresponding change in the x coordinate, between two distinct points on the line.
Equilibrium price	Equilibrium price refers to the price in a competitive market at which the quantity demanded and the quantity supplied are equal, there is neither a shortage nor a surplus, and there is no tendency for price to rise or fall.
Incidence	The ultimate economic effect of a tax on the real incomes of producers or consumers. Thus a sales tax may be paid by a retailer, but it is likely that the incidence falls upon the consumer.
Incentive	An incentive is any factor (financial or non-financial) that provides a motive for a particular course of action, or counts as a reason for preferring one choice to the alternatives.
Market price	Market price is an economic concept with commonplace familiarity; it is the price that a good or service is offered at, or will fetch, in the marketplace; it is of interest mainly in the study of microeconomics.
Factors of production	Economic resources: land, capital, labor, and entrepreneurial ability are called factors of production.
Operation	A standardized method or technique that is performed repetitively, often on different materials resulting in different finished goods is called an operation.
Labor	People's physical and mental talents and efforts that are used to help produce goods and services are called labor.
Inputs	The inputs used by a firm or an economy are the labor, raw materials, electricity and other resources it uses to produce its outputs.
Factor of production	Factor of production refers to economic resources used in production such as land, labor, and capital.
Business Week	Business Week is a business magazine published by McGraw-Hill. It was first published in 1929 under the direction of Malcolm Muir, who was serving as president of the McGraw-Hill Publishing company at the time. It is considered to be the standard both in industry and among students.
Economy	The income, expenditures, and resources that affect the cost of running a business and household are called an economy.
Opportunity cost	The cost of something in terms of opportunity foregone. The opportunity cost to a country of producing a unit more of a good, such as for export or to replace an import, is the quantity of some other good that could have been produced instead.
Economic profit	In Economics, a firm is said to be making an economic profit when its revenue exceeds the total opportunity cost of its inputs. It is said to be making an accounting profit if its revenues exceed the total price the firm pays for those inputs. This is sometimes referred to as producer's surplus.
Economic rent	Economic rent is an analytic term employed to distinguish the difference between the income

earned by an input or factor of production, and the cost of the factor of production.

License

A license in the sphere of Intellectual Property Rights (IPR) is a document, contract or agreement giving permission or the 'right' to a legally-definable entity to do something (such as manufacture a product or to use a service), or to apply something (such as a trademark), with the objective of achieving commercial gain.

Market value

Market value refers to the price of an asset agreed on between a willing buyer and a willing seller; the price an asset could demand if it is sold on the open market.

Wage

The payment for the service of a unit of labor, per unit time. In trade theory, it is the only payment to labor, usually unskilled labor. In empirical work, wage data may exclude other compenzation, which must be added to get the total cost of employment.

Lease

A contract for the possession and use of land or other property, including goods, on one side, and a recompense of rent or other income on the other is the lease.

Depreciation

Depreciation is an accounting and finance term for the method of attributing the cost of an asset across the useful life of the asset. Depreciation is a reduction in the value of a currency in floating exchange rate.

Net profit

Net profit is an accounting term which is commonly used in business. It is equal to the gross revenue for a given time period minus associated expenses.

Insurance

Insurance refers to a system by which individuals can reduce their exposure to risk of large losses by spreading the risks among a large number of persons.

Labor market

Any arrangement that brings buyers and sellers of labor services together to agree on conditions of work and pay is called a labor market.

Marginal cost

Marginal cost refers to the increase in cost that accompanies a unit increase in output; the partial derivative of the cost function with respect to output.

Present value

The value today of a stream of payments and/or receipts over time in the future and/or the past, converted to the present using an interest rate. If X t is the amount in period t and r the interest rate, then present value at time t=0 is V = ?T /t.

Policy

Similar to a script in that a policy can be a less than completely rational decision-making method. Involves the use of a pre-existing set of decision steps for any problem that presents itself.

Monopoly

A monopoly is defined as a persistent market situation where there is only one provider of a kind of product or service.

Consumption

In Keynesian economics consumption refers to personal consumption expenditure, i.e., the purchase of currently produced goods and services out of income, out of savings (net worth), or from borrowed funds. It refers to that part of disposable income that does not go to saving.

Allocate

Allocate refers to the assignment of income for various tax purposes. A multistate corporation's nonbusiness income usually is distributed to the state where the nonbusiness assets are located; it is not apportioned with the rest of the entity's income.

Applicant

In many tribunal and administrative law suits, the person who initiates the claim is called the applicant.

Capital

Capital generally refers to financial wealth, especially that used to start or maintain a business. In classical economics, capital is one of four factors of production, the others being land and labor and entrepreneurship.

Holder

A person in possession of a document of title or an instrument payable or indorsed to him,

his order, or to bearer is a holder.

Licensing	Licensing is a form of strategic alliance which involves the sale of a right to use certain proprietary knowledge (so called intellectual property) in a defined way.
Scarcity	Scarcity is defined as not having sufficient resources to produce enough to fulfill unlimited subjective wants. Alternatively, scarcity implies that not all of society's goals can be attained at the same time, so that trade-offs one good against others are made.
Artificial scarcity	Artificial scarcity is an economic term describing the scarcity of items even though the technology and production capacity exists to create an abundance. In economic terms, most non-rival goods (cable television, digital media) are artificially scarce, as one person's use does not diminish use by another.
Beneficiary	The person for whose benefit an insurance policy, trust, will, or contract is established is a beneficiary. In the case of a contract, the beneficiary is called a third-party beneficiary.
Public relations	Public relations refers to the management function that evaluates public attitudes, changes policies and procedures in response to the public's requests, and executes a program of action and information to earn public understanding and acceptance.
Expense	In accounting, an expense represents an event in which an asset is used up or a liability is incurred. In terms of the accounting equation, expenses reduce owners' equity.
Rent seeking	Rent seeking is the process by which an individual or firm seeks to gain through manipulation of the economic environment, rather than through trade and the production of added wealth.
Federal government	Federal government refers to the government of the United States, as distinct from the state and local governments.
Price support	Price support refers to government action to increase the price of a product, usually by buying it. May be associated with a price floor.
Cooperative	A business owned and controlled by the people who use it, producers, consumers, or workers with similar needs who pool their resources for mutual gain is called cooperative.
Subsidy	Subsidy refers to government financial assistance to a domestic producer.
Security	Security refers to a claim on the borrower future income that is sold by the borrower to the lender. A security is a type of transferable interest representing financial value.
Federal budget	The annual statement of the expenditures and tax revenues of the government of the United States together with the laws and regulations that approve and support those expenditures and taxes is the federal budget.
Economics	The social science dealing with the use of scarce resources to obtain the maximum satisfaction of society's virtually unlimited economic wants is an economics.
Budget	Budget refers to an account, usually for a year, of the planned expenditures and the expected receipts of an entity. For a government, the receipts are tax revenues.
Exporting	Selling products to another country is called exporting.
Domestic	From or in one's own country. A domestic producer is one that produces inside the home country. A domestic price is the price inside the home country. Opposite of 'foreign' or 'world.'.
Domestic price	The price of a good or service within a country, determined by domestic demand and supply is referred to as domestic price.
Factor price	Factor price refers to the price paid for the services of a unit of a primary factor of

Go to **Cram101.com** for the Practice Tests for this Chapter.

	production per unit time. Includes the wage or salary of labor and the rental prices of land and capital, and normal profits for the entrepreneur.
Margin	A deposit by a buyer in stocks with a seller or a stockbroker, as security to cover fluctuations in the market in reference to stocks that the buyer has purchased but for which he has not paid is a margin. Commodities are also traded on margin.
Economic forces	Forces that affect the availability, production, and distribution of a society's resources among competing users are referred to as economic forces.
Argument	The discussion by counsel for the respective parties of their contentions on the law and the facts of the case being tried in order to aid the jury in arriving at a correct and just conclusion is called argument.
Department of Energy	The Department of Energy is a Cabinet-level department of the United States government responsible for energy policy and nuclear safety. Its purview includes the nation's nuclear weapons program, nuclear reactor production for the United States Navy, energy conservation, energy-related research, radioactive waste disposal, and domestic energy production.
Intervention	Intervention refers to an activity in which a government buys or sells its currency in the foreign exchange market in order to affect its currency's exchange rate.
Market system	All the product and resource markets of a market economy and the relationships among them are called a market system.
Free market	A free market is a market where price is determined by the unregulated interchange of supply and demand rather than set by artificial means.
Contract	A contract is a "promise" or an "agreement" that is enforced or recognized by the law. In the civil law, a contract is considered to be part of the general law of obligations.
Entitlement program	Requires the federal government to pay benefits to anyone who meets the eligibility requirements of the program are referred to as entitlement program.
Coupon	In finance, a coupon is "attached" to a bond, either physically (as with old bonds) or electronically. Each coupon represents a predetermined payment promized to the bond-holder in return for his or her loan of money to the bond-issuer. .
Inelastic	Inelastic refers to having an elasticity less than one. For a price elasticity of demand, this means that expenditure falls as price falls. For an income elasticity, it means that expenditure share falls with income.
Accounting	A system that collects and processes financial information about an organization and reports that information to decision makers is referred to as accounting.

Go to **Cram101.com** for the Practice Tests for this Chapter.

Market price	Market price is an economic concept with commonplace familiarity; it is the price that a good or service is offered at, or will fetch, in the marketplace; it is of interest mainly in the study of microeconomics.
Market	A market is, as defined in economics, a social arrangement that allows buyers and sellers to discover information and carry out a voluntary exchange of goods or services.
Firm	An organization that employs resources to produce a good or service for profit and owns and operates one or more plants is referred to as a firm.
Profit	Profit refers to the return to the resource entrepreneurial ability; total revenue minus total cost.
Revenue	Revenue is a U.S. business term for the amount of money that a company receives from its activities, mostly from sales of products and/or services to customers.
Marginal revenue	Marginal revenue refers to the change in total revenue obtained by selling one additional unit.
Marginal cost	Marginal cost refers to the increase in cost that accompanies a unit increase in output; the partial derivative of the cost function with respect to output.
Incentive	An incentive is any factor (financial or non-financial) that provides a motive for a particular course of action, or counts as a reason for preferring one choice to the alternatives.
Competitive firm	Competitive firm refers to a firm without market power, with no ability to alter the market price of the goods it produces.
Demand curve	Demand curve refers to the graph of quantity demanded as a function of price, normally downward sloping, straight or curved, and drawn with quantity on the horizontal axis and price on the vertical axis.
Monopoly	A monopoly is defined as a persistent market situation where there is only one provider of a kind of product or service.
Competitor	Other organizations in the same industry or type of business that provide a good or service to the same set of customers is referred to as a competitor.
Elasticity	In economics, elasticity is the ratio of the incremental percentage change in one variable with respect to an incremental percentage change in another variable. Elasticity is usually expressed as a positive number (i.e., an absolute value) when the sign is already clear from context.
Elastic demand	Elastic demand refers to product or resource demand whose price elasticity is greater than 1. This means the resulting change in quantity demanded is greater than the percentage change in price.
Inelastic demand	Inelastic demand refers to product or resource demand for which the elasticity coefficient for price is less than 1. This means the resulting percentage change in quantity demanded is less than the percentage change in price. In other words, consumers are relatively less sensitive to changes in price.
Total cost	The sum of fixed cost and variable cost is referred to as total cost.
Inelastic	Inelastic refers to having an elasticity less than one. For a price elasticity of demand, this means that expenditure falls as price falls. For an income elasticity, it means that expenditure share falls with income.
Markup pricing	Markup pricing refers to the pricing method used by many firms in situations of imperfect competition; under this method they estimate average cost and then add some fixed percentage

Go to **Cram101.com** for the Practice Tests for this Chapter.

Go to **Cram101.com** for the Practice Tests for this Chapter.
And, **NEVER** highlight a book again!

	to that cost in order to reach the price they charge.
Cost curve	A cost curve is a graph of the costs of production as a function of total quantity produced. In a free market economy, productively efficient firms use these curves to find the optimal point of production, where they make the most profits.
Markup	Markup is a term used in marketing to indicate how much the price of a product is above the cost of producing and distributing the product.
Marginal revenue curve	A graph of the relationship between the change in total revenue and the quantity sold is referred to as the marginal revenue curve.
Policy	Similar to a script in that a policy can be a less than completely rational decision-making method. Involves the use of a pre-existing set of decision steps for any problem that presents itself.
Yield	The interest rate that equates a future value or an annuity to a given present value is a yield.
Industry	A group of firms that produce identical or similar products is an industry. It is also used specifically to refer to an area of economic production focused on manufacturing which involves large amounts of capital investment before any profit can be realized, also called "heavy industry".
Value judgment	Value judgment refers to an opinion of what is desirable or undesirable; belief regarding what ought or ought not to be.
Welfare	Welfare refers to the economic well being of an individual, group, or economy. For individuals, it is conceptualized by a utility function. For groups, including countries and the world, it is a tricky philosophical concept, since individuals fare differently.
Deadweight loss	Deadweight loss refers to the net loss in economic welfare that is caused by a tariff or tax, defined as the total losses to those who lose, minus the total gains to those who gain.
Willingness to pay	Willingness to pay refers to the largest amount of money that an individual or group could pay, along with a change in policy, without being made worse off.
Patent	The legal right to the proceeds from and control over the use of an invented product or process, granted for a fixed period of time, usually 20 years. Patent is one form of intellectual property that is subject of the TRIPS agreement.
Innovation	Innovation refers to the first commercially successful introduction of a new product, the use of a new method of production, or the creation of a new form of business organization.
Research and development	The use of resources for the deliberate discovery of new information and ways of doing things, together with the application of that information in inventing new products or processes is referred to as research and development.
Gain	In finance, gain is a profit or an increase in value of an investment such as a stock or bond. Gain is calculated by fair market value or the proceeds from the sale of the investment minus the sum of the purchase price and all costs associated with it.
Balance	In banking and accountancy, the outstanding balance is the amount of money owned, (or due), that remains in a deposit account (or a loan account) at a given date, after all past remittances, payments and withdrawal have been accounted for. It can be positive (then, in the balance sheet of a firm, it is an asset) or negative (a liability).
Natural monopoly	Natural monopoly refers to an industry in which economies of scale are so great that a single firm can produce the product at a lower average total cost than would be possible if more than one firm produced the product.

Go to **Cram101.com** for the Practice Tests for this Chapter.

Profit maximization	Search by a firm for the product quantity, quality, and price that gives that firm the highest possible profit is profit maximization.
Fixed cost	The cost that a firm bears if it does not produce at all and that is independent of its output. The presence of a fixed cost tends to imply increasing returns to scale. Contrasts with variable cost.
Technology	The body of knowledge and techniques that can be used to combine economic resources to produce goods and services is called technology.
Service	Service refers to a "non tangible product" that is not embodied in a physical good and that typically effects some change in another product, person, or institution. Contrasts with good.
Subsidy	Subsidy refers to government financial assistance to a domestic producer.
Average cost	Average cost is equal to total cost divided by the number of goods produced (Quantity-Q). It is also equal to the sum of average variable costs (total variable costs divided by Q) plus average fixed costs (total fixed costs divided by Q).
Public utility	A firm that produces an essential good or service, has obtained from a government the right to be the sole supplier of the good or service in the area, and is regulated by that government to prevent the abuse of its monopoly power is a public utility.
Utility	Utility refers to the want-satisfying power of a good or service; the satisfaction or pleasure a consumer obtains from the consumption of a good or service.
Operation	A standardized method or technique that is performed repetitively, often on different materials resulting in different finished goods is called an operation.
Bureaucracy	Bureaucracy refers to an organization with many layers of managers who set rules and regulations and oversee all decisions.
Hearing	A hearing is a proceeding before a court or other decision-making body or officer. A hearing is generally distinguished from a trial in that it is usually shorter and often less formal.
Efficient scale	The quantity of output that minimizes average total cost is referred to as efficient scale.
Minimum efficient scale	The smallest output of a firm consistent with minimum average cost. In small countries, in some industries the level of demand in autarky is not sufficient to support minimum efficient scale.
Production	The creation of finished goods and services using the factors of production: land, labor, capital, entrepreneurship, and knowledge.
Domestic	From or in one's own country. A domestic producer is one that produces inside the home country. A domestic price is the price inside the home country. Opposite of 'foreign' or 'world.'.
Intervention	Intervention refers to an activity in which a government buys or sells its currency in the foreign exchange market in order to affect its currency's exchange rate.
Regulation	Regulation refers to restrictions state and federal laws place on business with regard to the conduct of its activities.
Cartel	Cartel refers to a group of firms that seeks to raise the price of a good by restricting its supply. The term is usually used for international groups, especially involving state-owned firms and/or governments.
Antitrust	Government intervention to alter market structure or prevent abuse of market power is called antitrust.

Federal trade commission	The commission of five members established by the Federal Trade Commission Act of 1914 to investigate unfair competitive practices of firms, to hold hearings on the complaints of such practices, and to issue cease-and-desist orders when firms were found guilty of unfair practices.
Cost advantage	Possession of a lower cost of production or operation than a competing firm or country is cost advantage.
De Beers	In 1994 De Beers was charged by the United States Justice Department with antitrust violations for conspiring to fix prices for industrial diamonds. On 14 July 2004 De Beers pleaded guilty to the charges and paid a $10 million fine. They have historically held a near-total monopoly in the diamond trade.
Scarcity	Scarcity is defined as not having sufficient resources to produce enough to fulfill unlimited subjective wants. Alternatively, scarcity implies that not all of society's goals can be attained at the same time, so that trade-offs one good against others are made.
Quota	A government-imposed restriction on quantity, or sometimes on total value, used to restrict the import of something to a specific quantity is called a quota.
Wholesale	According to the United Nations Statistics Division Wholesale is the resale of new and used goods to retailers, to industrial, commercial, institutional or professional users, or to other wholesalers, or involves acting as an agent or broker in buying merchandise for, or selling merchandise, to such persons or companies.
Buyer	A buyer refers to a role in the buying center with formal authority and responsibility to select the supplier and negotiate the terms of the contract.
Auction	A preexisting business model that operates successfully on the Internet by announcing an item for sale and permitting multiple purchasers to bid on them under specified rules and condition is an auction.
Dealer	People who link buyers with sellers by buying and selling securities at stated prices are referred to as a dealer.
Bid	A bid price is a price offered by a buyer when he/she buys a good. In the context of stock trading on a stock exchange, the bid price is the highest price a buyer of a stock is willing to pay for a share of that given stock.
Net loss	Net loss refers to the amount by which expenses exceed revenues. The difference between income received and expenses, when expenses are greater.
Supply	Supply is the aggregate amount of any material good that can be called into being at a certain price point; it comprises one half of the equation of supply and demand. In classical economic theory, a curve representing supply is one of the factors that produce price.
Cost function	The relationship, expressed as an equation, between a cost and a one or more variables is the cost function. In choosing a cost function both economic plausibility and goodness fit are relevant. It measures how good any particular solution is.

101

Market price	Market price is an economic concept with commonplace familiarity; it is the price that a good or service is offered at, or will fetch, in the marketplace; it is of interest mainly in the study of microeconomics.
Competitor	Other organizations in the same industry or type of business that provide a good or service to the same set of customers is referred to as a competitor.
Market	A market is, as defined in economics, a social arrangement that allows buyers and sellers to discover information and carry out a voluntary exchange of goods or services.
Firm	An organization that employs resources to produce a good or service for profit and owns and operates one or more plants is referred to as a firm.
Industry	A group of firms that produce identical or similar products is an industry. It is also used specifically to refer to an area of economic production focused on manufacturing which involves large amounts of capital investment before any profit can be realized, also called "heavy industry".
Competitive firm	Competitive firm refers to a firm without market power, with no ability to alter the market price of the goods it produces.
Monopoly power	Monopoly power is an example of market failure which occurs when one or more of the participants has the ability to influence the price or other outcomes in some general or specialized market.
Monopoly	A monopoly is defined as a persistent market situation where there is only one provider of a kind of product or service.
Option	A contract that gives the purchaser the option to buy or sell the underlying financial instrument at a specified price, called the exercise price or strike price, within a specific period of time.
Perfectly competitive	Perfectly competitive is an economic agent, group of agents, model or analysis that is characterized by perfect competition. Contrasts with imperfectly competitive.
Market power	The ability of a single economic actor to have a substantial influence on market prices is market power.
Price discrimination	Price discrimination refers to the sale by a firm to buyers at two different prices. When this occurs internationally and the lower price is charged for export, it is regarded as dumping.
Discount	The difference between the face value of a bond and its selling price, when a bond is sold for less than its face value it's referred to as a discount.
Willingness to pay	Willingness to pay refers to the largest amount of money that an individual or group could pay, along with a change in policy, without being made worse off.
Demand curve	Demand curve refers to the graph of quantity demanded as a function of price, normally downward sloping, straight or curved, and drawn with quantity on the horizontal axis and price on the vertical axis.
Profit	Profit refers to the return to the resource entrepreneurial ability; total revenue minus total cost.
Yield	The interest rate that equates a future value or an annuity to a given present value is a yield.
Competitive market	A market in which no buyer or seller has market power is called a competitive market.
Marginal cost	Marginal cost refers to the increase in cost that accompanies a unit increase in output; the

	partial derivative of the cost function with respect to output.
Pareto efficiency	A condition in which no change is possible that will make some members of society better off without making some other members of society worse off is referred to as pareto efficiency. It is a central concept in economics with broad applications in game theory, engineering and the social sciences.
Resource allocation	Resource allocation refers to the manner in which an economy distributes its resources among the potential uses so as to produce a particular set of final goods.
Distribution	Distribution in economics, the manner in which total output and income is distributed among individuals or factors.
Standing	Standing refers to the legal requirement that anyone seeking to challenge a particular action in court must demonstrate that such action substantially affects his legitimate interests before he will be entitled to bring suit.
Incentive	An incentive is any factor (financial or non-financial) that provides a motive for a particular course of action, or counts as a reason for preferring one choice to the alternatives.
Economics	The social science dealing with the use of scarce resources to obtain the maximum satisfaction of society's virtually unlimited economic wants is an economics.
Jargon	Jargon is terminology, much like slang, that relates to a specific activity, profession, or group. It develops as a kind of shorthand, to express ideas that are frequently discussed between members of a group, and can also have the effect of distinguishing those belonging to a group from those who are not.
Marginal benefit	Marginal benefit refers to the extra benefit of consuming 1 more unit of some good or service; the change in total benefit when 1 more unit is consumed.
Balance	In banking and accountancy, the outstanding balance is the amount of money owned, (or due), that remains in a deposit account (or a loan account) at a given date, after all past remittances, payments and withdrawal have been accounted for. It can be positive (then, in the balance sheet of a firm, it is an asset) or negative (a liability).
Purchasing	Purchasing refers to the function in a firm that searches for quality material resources, finds the best suppliers, and negotiates the best price for goods and services.
Level of service	The degree of service provided to the customer by self, limited, and full-service retailers is referred to as the level of service.
Service	Service refers to a "non tangible product" that is not embodied in a physical good and that typically effects some change in another product, person, or institution. Contrasts with good.
Marginal revenue	Marginal revenue refers to the change in total revenue obtained by selling one additional unit.
Revenue	Revenue is a U.S. business term for the amount of money that a company receives from its activities, mostly from sales of products and/or services to customers.
Elasticity	In economics, elasticity is the ratio of the incremental percentage change in one variable with respect to an incremental percentage change in another variable. Elasticity is usually expressed as a positive number (i.e., an absolute value) when the sign is already clear from context.
Elastic demand	Elastic demand refers to product or resource demand whose price elasticity is greater than 1. This means the resulting change in quantity demanded is greater than the percentage change in price.

Total demand	Total demand refers to the demand schedule or the demand curve of all buyers of a good or service; also called market demand.
Journal	Book of original entry, in which transactions are recorded in a general ledger system, is referred to as a journal.
Economic analysis	The process of deriving economic principles from relevant economic facts are called economic analysis. It is the comparison, with money as the index, of those costs and benefits to the wider economy that can be reasonably quantified, including all social costs and benefits of a project.
Inelastic	Inelastic refers to having an elasticity less than one. For a price elasticity of demand, this means that expenditure falls as price falls. For an income elasticity, it means that expenditure share falls with income.
Exchange rate	Exchange rate refers to the price at which one country's currency trades for another, typically on the exchange market.
Exchange	The trade of things of value between buyer and seller so that each is better off after the trade is called the exchange.
Pricing strategy	The process in which the price of a product can be determined and is decided upon is a pricing strategy.
Correlation	A correlation is the measure of the extent to which two economic or statistical variables move together, normalized so that its values range from -1 to +1. It is defined as the covariance of the two variables divided by the square root of the product of their variances.
Vendor	A person who sells property to a vendee is a vendor. The words vendor and vendee are more commonly applied to the seller and purchaser of real estate, and the words seller and buyer are more commonly applied to the seller and purchaser of personal property.
Acquisition	A company's purchase of the property and obligations of another company is an acquisition.
Preference	The act of a debtor in paying or securing one or more of his creditors in a manner more favorable to them than to other creditors or to the exclusion of such other creditors is a preference. In the absence of statute, a preference is perfectly good, but to be legal it must be bona fide, and not a mere subterfuge of the debtor to secure a future benefit to himself or to prevent the application of his property to his debts.
Policy	Similar to a script in that a policy can be a less than completely rational decision-making method. Involves the use of a pre-existing set of decision steps for any problem that presents itself.
Valuation	In finance, valuation is the process of estimating the market value of a financial asset or liability. They can be done on assets (for example, investments in marketable securities such as stocks, options, business enterprises, or intangible assets such as patents and trademarks) or on liabilities (e.g., Bonds issued by a company).
Microsoft	Microsoft is a multinational computer technology corporation with 2004 global annual sales of US$39.79 billion and 71,553 employees in 102 countries and regions as of July 2006. It develops, manufactures, licenses, and supports a wide range of software products for computing devices.
Tariff	A tax imposed by a nation on an imported good is called a tariff.
Users	Users refer to people in the organization who actually use the product or service purchased by the buying center.
Complementary good	A complementary good refers to a product or service that is used together with another good. When the price of one falls, the demand for the other increases. Cameras and film are

considered complementary goods.

Cost curve	A cost curve is a graph of the costs of production as a function of total quantity produced. In a free market economy, productively efficient firms use these curves to find the optimal point of production, where they make the most profits.
Disney	Disney is one of the largest media and entertainment corporations in the world. Founded on October 16, 1923 by brothers Walt and Roy Disney as a small animation studio, today it is one of the largest Hollywood studios and also owns nine theme parks and several television networks, including the American Broadcasting Company (ABC).
Slope	The slope of a line in the plane containing the x and y axes is generally represented by the letter m, and is defined as the change in the y coordinate divided by the corresponding change in the x coordinate, between two distinct points on the line.
Monopolistic competition	Monopolistic competition refers to a market structure in which there are many sellers each producing a differentiated product.
Transactions cost	Any cost associated with bringing buyers and sellers together is referred to as transactions cost.
Brand	A name, symbol, or design that identifies the goods or services of one seller or group of sellers and distinguishes them from the goods and services of competitors is a brand.
Trademark	A distinctive word, name, symbol, device, or combination thereof, which enables consumers to identify favored products or services and which may find protection under state or federal law is a trademark.
Consideration	Consideration in contract law, a basic requirement for an enforceable agreement under traditional contract principles, defined in this text as legal value, bargained for and given in exchange for an act or promise. In corporation law, cash or property contributed to a corporation in exchange for shares, or a promise to contribute such cash or property.
Production	The creation of finished goods and services using the factors of production: land, labor, capital, entrepreneurship, and knowledge.
Product differentiation	A strategy in which one firm's product is distinguished from competing products by means of its design, related services, quality, location, or other attributes is called product differentiation.
Pure competition	A market structure in which a very large number of firms sells a standardized product, into which entry is very easy, in which the individual seller has no control over the product price, and in which there is no non-price competition is pure competition.
Pure monopoly	A market structure in which one firm sells a unique product, into which entry is blocked, in which the single firm has considerable control over product price, and in which non-price competition may or may not be found is called pure monopoly.
Strategic choice	Strategic choice refers to an organization's strategy; the ways an organization will attempt to fulfill its mission and achieve its long-term goals.
Technology	The body of knowledge and techniques that can be used to combine economic resources to produce goods and services is called technology.
Average cost	Average cost is equal to total cost divided by the number of goods produced (Quantity-Q). It is also equal to the sum of average variable costs (total variable costs divided by Q) plus average fixed costs (total fixed costs divided by Q).
Argument	The discussion by counsel for the respective parties of their contentions on the law and the facts of the case being tried in order to aid the jury in arriving at a correct and just conclusion is called argument.

Competitive equilibrium	The balancing of supply and demand in a market or economy characterized by perfect competition is competitive equilibrium.
Efficient scale	The quantity of output that minimizes average total cost is referred to as efficient scale.
Operation	A standardized method or technique that is performed repetitively, often on different materials resulting in different finished goods is called an operation.
Market share	That fraction of an industry's output accounted for by an individual firm or group of firms is called market share.
Appeal	Appeal refers to the act of asking an appellate court to overturn a decision after the trial court's final judgment has been entered.
Gain	In finance, gain is a profit or an increase in value of an investment such as a stock or bond. Gain is calculated by fair market value or the proceeds from the sale of the investment minus the sum of the purchase price and all costs associated with it.
Commodity	Could refer to any good, but in trade a commodity is usually a raw material or primary product that enters into international trade, such as metals or basic agricultural products.
Free entry	Free entry refers to the assumption that new firms are permitted to enter an industry without substantial barriers to entry. Together with free exit, it implies that economic profit must be zero in equilibrium.

Go to **Cram101.com** for the Practice Tests for this Chapter.

155

Monopoly	A monopoly is defined as a persistent market situation where there is only one provider of a kind of product or service.
Marginal revenue	Marginal revenue refers to the change in total revenue obtained by selling one additional unit.
Marginal cost	Marginal cost refers to the increase in cost that accompanies a unit increase in output; the partial derivative of the cost function with respect to output.
Revenue	Revenue is a U.S. business term for the amount of money that a company receives from its activities, mostly from sales of products and/or services to customers.
Profit	Profit refers to the return to the resource entrepreneurial ability; total revenue minus total cost.
Market	A market is, as defined in economics, a social arrangement that allows buyers and sellers to discover information and carry out a voluntary exchange of goods or services.
Firm	An organization that employs resources to produce a good or service for profit and owns and operates one or more plants is referred to as a firm.
Marginal product	In a production function, the marginal product of a factor is the increase in output due to a unit increase in the input of the factor; that is, the partial derivative of the production function with respect to the factor.
Marginal revenue product	Marginal revenue product refers to the additional revenue generated by the extra output from employing one more unit of a factor of production. In a competitive industry this equals the marginal value product.
Perfectly elastic	Perfectly elastic refers to a supply or demand curve with a price elasticity of infinity, implying that the supply or demand curve as usually drawn is horizontal. A small open economy faces perfectly elastic demand for its exports and supply of its imports.
Competitive firm	Competitive firm refers to a firm without market power, with no ability to alter the market price of the goods it produces.
Demand curve	Demand curve refers to the graph of quantity demanded as a function of price, normally downward sloping, straight or curved, and drawn with quantity on the horizontal axis and price on the vertical axis.
Slope	The slope of a line in the plane containing the x and y axes is generally represented by the letter m, and is defined as the change in the y coordinate divided by the corresponding change in the x coordinate, between two distinct points on the line.
Value of the marginal product	The marginal product of an input times the price of the output is a value of the marginal product.
Paradox	As used in economics, paradox means something unexpected, rather than the more extreme normal meaning of something seemingly impossible. Some paradoxes are just theoretical results that go against what one thinks of as normal.
Short run	Short run refers to a period of time that permits an increase or decrease in current production volume with existing capacity, but one that is too short to permit enlargement of that capacity itself (eg, the building of new plants, training of additional workers, etc.).
Margin	A deposit by a buyer in stocks with a seller or a stockbroker, as security to cover fluctuations in the market in reference to stocks that the buyer has purchased but for which he has not paid is a margin. Commodities are also traded on margin.
Monopsony	A market structure in which there is a single buyer is referred to as monopsony.

Commodity	Could refer to any good, but in trade a commodity is usually a raw material or primary product that enters into international trade, such as metals or basic agricultural products.
Factor market	Any place where factors of production, resources, are bought and sold is referred to as factor market.
Factor price	Factor price refers to the price paid for the services of a unit of a primary factor of production per unit time. Includes the wage or salary of labor and the rental prices of land and capital, and normal profits for the entrepreneur.
Supply curve	Supply curve refers to the graph of quantity supplied as a function of price, normally upward sloping, straight or curved, and drawn with quantity on the horizontal axis and price on the vertical axis.
Supply	Supply is the aggregate amount of any material good that can be called into being at a certain price point; it comprises one half of the equation of supply and demand. In classical economic theory, a curve representing supply is one of the factors that produce price.
Factor supply curve	The factor supply curve displays the quantity of a factor supplied at alternative factor prices. While all factors of production, or scarce resources, including labor, capital, land, and entrepreneurship, have a factor supply curve, labor is the factor most often analyzed.
Price taker	Price taker refers to an economic entity that is too small relative to a market to affect its price, and that therefore must take that price as given in making its own decisions. Applies to all buyers in sellers in markets that are perfectly competitive.
Total cost	The sum of fixed cost and variable cost is referred to as total cost.
Competitive market	A market in which no buyer or seller has market power is called a competitive market.
Equilibrium wage	The wage rate at which the quantity of labor supplied in a given time period equals the quantity of labor demanded is an equilibrium wage.
Supply of labor	Supply of labor refers to the relationship between the quantity of labor supplied by employees and the real wage rate when all other influences on work plans remain the same.
Minimum wage	The lowest wage employers may legally pay for an hour of work is the minimum wage.
Labor	People's physical and mental talents and efforts that are used to help produce goods and services are called labor.
Wage	The payment for the service of a unit of labor, per unit time. In trade theory, it is the only payment to labor, usually unskilled labor. In empirical work, wage data may exclude other compenzation, which must be added to get the total cost of employment.
Labor market	Any arrangement that brings buyers and sellers of labor services together to agree on conditions of work and pay is called a labor market.
Price ceiling	Price ceiling refers to a government-imposed upper limit on the price that may be charged for a product. If that limit is binding, it implies a situation of excess demand and shortage.
Policy	Similar to a script in that a policy can be a less than completely rational decision-making method. Involves the use of a pre-existing set of decision steps for any problem that presents itself.
Imperfect competition	Any departure from perfect competition. However, imperfect competition usually refers to one of the market structures other than perfect competition.
Buyer	A buyer refers to a role in the buying center with formal authority and responsibility to select the supplier and negotiate the terms of the contract.

Go to **Cram101.com** for the Practice Tests for this Chapter.

Production	The creation of finished goods and services using the factors of production: land, labor, capital, entrepreneurship, and knowledge.
Production function	Production function refers to a function that specifies the output in an industry for all combinations of inputs.
Interest	In finance and economics, interest is the price paid by a borrower for the use of a lender's money. In other words, interest is the amount of paid to "rent" money for a period of time.
Marginal revenue curve	A graph of the relationship between the change in total revenue and the quantity sold is referred to as the marginal revenue curve.
Cost curve	A cost curve is a graph of the costs of production as a function of total quantity produced. In a free market economy, productively efficient firms use these curves to find the optimal point of production, where they make the most profits.
Factor of production	Factor of production refers to economic resources used in production such as land, labor, and capital.
Markup	Markup is a term used in marketing to indicate how much the price of a product is above the cost of producing and distributing the product.
Inelastic	Inelastic refers to having an elasticity less than one. For a price elasticity of demand, this means that expenditure falls as price falls. For an income elasticity, it means that expenditure share falls with income.

Go to **Cram101.com** for the Practice Tests for this Chapter.

Competitor	Other organizations in the same industry or type of business that provide a good or service to the same set of customers is referred to as a competitor.
Market	A market is, as defined in economics, a social arrangement that allows buyers and sellers to discover information and carry out a voluntary exchange of goods or services.
Firm	An organization that employs resources to produce a good or service for profit and owns and operates one or more plants is referred to as a firm.
Duopoly	A true duopoly is a form of oligopoly where only two producers exist in a market. In reality, this definition is generally eased whereby two firms must only have dominant control over a market.
Strategic interaction	A situation in oligopolistic markets in which each firm's business strategies depend upon its rival's plans. A formal analysis of strategic interaction is given in game theory.
Homogeneous	In the context of procurement/purchasing, homogeneous is used to describe goods that do not vary in their essential characteristic irrespective of the source of supply.
Variable	A variable is something measured by a number; it is used to analyze what happens to other things when the size of that number changes.
Interest	In finance and economics, interest is the price paid by a borrower for the use of a lender's money. In other words, interest is the amount of paid to "rent" money for a period of time.
Homogeneous Product	Homogeneous product refers to the product of an industry in which the outputs of different firms are indistinguishable. Contrasts with differentiated product.
Leadership	Management merely consists of leadership applied to business situations; or in other words: management forms a sub-set of the broader process of leadership.
Industry	A group of firms that produce identical or similar products is an industry. It is also used specifically to refer to an area of economic production focused on manufacturing which involves large amounts of capital investment before any profit can be realized, also called "heavy industry".
Equilibrium price	Equilibrium price refers to the price in a competitive market at which the quantity demanded and the quantity supplied are equal, there is neither a shortage nor a surplus, and there is no tendency for price to rise or fall.
Profit	Profit refers to the return to the resource entrepreneurial ability; total revenue minus total cost.
Production	The creation of finished goods and services using the factors of production: land, labor, capital, entrepreneurship, and knowledge.
Marginal revenue	Marginal revenue refers to the change in total revenue obtained by selling one additional unit.
Marginal cost	Marginal cost refers to the increase in cost that accompanies a unit increase in output; the partial derivative of the cost function with respect to output.
Revenue	Revenue is a U.S. business term for the amount of money that a company receives from its activities, mostly from sales of products and/or services to customers.
Oligopoly	A market structure in which there are a small number of sellers, at least some of whose individual decisions about price or quantity matter to the others is an oligopoly.
Reaction curve	The graph of a reaction function is a reaction curve.
Price leadership	An informal method that firms in an oligopoly may employ to set the price of their product: One firm is the first to announce a change in price, and the other firms soon announce

163

identical or similar changes is called price leadership.

Demand curve	Demand curve refers to the graph of quantity demanded as a function of price, normally downward sloping, straight or curved, and drawn with quantity on the horizontal axis and price on the vertical axis.
Residual	Residual payments can refer to an ongoing stream of payments in respect of the completion of past achievements.
Supply	Supply is the aggregate amount of any material good that can be called into being at a certain price point; it comprises one half of the equation of supply and demand. In classical economic theory, a curve representing supply is one of the factors that produce price.
Supply curve	Supply curve refers to the graph of quantity supplied as a function of price, normally upward sloping, straight or curved, and drawn with quantity on the horizontal axis and price on the vertical axis.
Marginal revenue curve	A graph of the relationship between the change in total revenue and the quantity sold is referred to as the marginal revenue curve.
Cost function	The relationship, expressed as an equation, between a cost and a one or more variables is the cost function. In choosing a cost function both economic plausibility and goodness fit are relevant. It measures how good any particular solution is.
Cost curve	A cost curve is a graph of the costs of production as a function of total quantity produced. In a free market economy, productively efficient firms use these curves to find the optimal point of production, where they make the most profits.
Monopoly	A monopoly is defined as a persistent market situation where there is only one provider of a kind of product or service.
Investment	Investment refers to spending for the production and accumulation of capital and additions to inventories. In a financial sense, buying an asset with the expectation of making a return.
Market price	Market price is an economic concept with commonplace familiarity; it is the price that a good or service is offered at, or will fetch, in the marketplace; it is of interest mainly in the study of microeconomics.
Yield	The interest rate that equates a future value or an annuity to a given present value is a yield.
Reaction function	Reaction function refers to the function specifying the choice of a strategic variable by one economic agent as a function of the choice of another agent. Most familiar specifying output choices of firms in a Cournot duopoly.
Confirmed	When the seller's bank agrees to assume liability on the letter of credit issued by the buyer's bank the transaction is confirmed. The term means that the credit is not only backed up by the issuing foreign bank, but that payment is also guaranteed by the notifying American bank.
Appeal	Appeal refers to the act of asking an appellate court to overturn a decision after the trial court's final judgment has been entered.
Market share	That fraction of an industry's output accounted for by an individual firm or group of firms is called market share.
Competitive bidding	A situation where two or more companies submit bids for a product, service, or project to a potential buyer is competitive bidding.
Collusion	Collusion refers to cooperation among firms to raise price and otherwise increase their profits.

Cartel	Cartel refers to a group of firms that seeks to raise the price of a good by restricting its supply. The term is usually used for international groups, especially involving state-owned firms and/or governments.
Cost advantage	Possession of a lower cost of production or operation than a competing firm or country is cost advantage.
Slope	The slope of a line in the plane containing the x and y axes is generally represented by the letter m, and is defined as the change in the y coordinate divided by the corresponding change in the x coordinate, between two distinct points on the line.
Quota	A government-imposed restriction on quantity, or sometimes on total value, used to restrict the import of something to a specific quantity is called a quota.
Monopoly profit	In economics, a firm is said to reap monopoly profit when a lack of viable market competition allows it to set its prices above the equilibrium price for a good or service without losing profits to competitors.
Interest rate	The rate of return on bonds, loans, or deposits. When one speaks of 'the' interest rate, it is usually in a model where there is only one.
Matching	Matching refers to an accounting concept that establishes when expenses are recognized. Expenses are matched with the revenues they helped to generate and are recognized when those revenues are recognized.
Export	In economics, an export is any good or commodity, shipped or otherwise transported out of a country, province, town to another part of the world in a legitimate fashion, typically for use in trade or sale.
Voluntary export restraint	Voluntary export restraint refers to a restriction on a country's imports that is achieved by negotiating with the foreign exporting country for it to restrict its exports. The restraint agreement may be concluded at either industry or government level. In the latter case, sometimes referred to as an orderly marketing arrangement.
Tariff	A tax imposed by a nation on an imported good is called a tariff.
Policy	Similar to a script in that a policy can be a less than completely rational decision-making method. Involves the use of a pre-existing set of decision steps for any problem that presents itself.
Competitive equilibrium	The balancing of supply and demand in a market or economy characterized by perfect competition is competitive equilibrium.
Cournot model	A Cournot model is a two-firm industry in which a series of output-adjustment decisions leads to a final level of output somewhere between the output that would prevail if the market were organized competitively and the output that would be set by a monopoly.
Elasticity	In economics, elasticity is the ratio of the incremental percentage change in one variable with respect to an incremental percentage change in another variable. Elasticity is usually expressed as a positive number (i.e., an absolute value) when the sign is already clear from context.

Go to **Cram101.com** for the Practice Tests for this Chapter.

Economic agents	Economic agents refers to individuals who engage in production, exchange, specialization, and consumption.
Game theory	The modeling of strategic interactions among agents, used in economic models where the numbers of interacting agents is small enough that each has a perceptible influence on the others is called game theory.
Agent	A person who makes economic decisions for another economic actor. A hired manager operates as an agent for a firm's owner.
Strategic interaction	A situation in oligopolistic markets in which each firm's business strategies depend upon its rival's plans. A formal analysis of strategic interaction is given in game theory.
Negotiation	Negotiation is the process whereby interested parties resolve disputes, agree upon courses of action, bargain for individual or collective advantage, and/or attempt to craft outcomes which serve their mutual interests.
Context	The effect of the background under which a message often takes on more and richer meaning is a context. Context is especially important in cross-cultural interactions because some cultures are said to be high context or low context.
Nash equilibrium	The Nash equilibrium is a kind of solution concept of a game involving two or more players, where no player has anything to gain by changing only his or her own strategy unilaterally.
Firm	An organization that employs resources to produce a good or service for profit and owns and operates one or more plants is referred to as a firm.
Profit	Profit refers to the return to the resource entrepreneurial ability; total revenue minus total cost.
Trust	An arrangement in which shareholders of independent firms agree to give up their stock in exchange for trust certificates that entitle them to a share of the trust's common profits.
Cartel	Cartel refers to a group of firms that seeks to raise the price of a good by restricting its supply. The term is usually used for international groups, especially involving state-owned firms and/or governments.
Quota	A government-imposed restriction on quantity, or sometimes on total value, used to restrict the import of something to a specific quantity is called a quota.
Marginal cost	Marginal cost refers to the increase in cost that accompanies a unit increase in output; the partial derivative of the cost function with respect to output.
Price war	Price war refers to successive and continued decreases in the prices charged by firms in an oligopolistic industry. Each firm lowers its price below rivals' prices, hoping to increase its sales and revenues at its rivals' expense.
Regulation	Regulation refers to restrictions state and federal laws place on business with regard to the conduct of its activities.
Antitrust	Government intervention to alter market structure or prevent abuse of market power is called antitrust.
Market share	That fraction of an industry's output accounted for by an individual firm or group of firms is called market share.
Market	A market is, as defined in economics, a social arrangement that allows buyers and sellers to discover information and carry out a voluntary exchange of goods or services.
Economics	The social science dealing with the use of scarce resources to obtain the maximum satisfaction of society's virtually unlimited economic wants is an economics.

Committee	A long-lasting, sometimes permanent team in the organization structure created to deal with tasks that recur regularly is the committee.
Journal	Book of original entry, in which transactions are recorded in a general ledger system, is referred to as a journal.
Competitor	Other organizations in the same industry or type of business that provide a good or service to the same set of customers is referred to as a competitor.
Promotion	Promotion refers to all the techniques sellers use to motivate people to buy products or services. An attempt by marketers to inform people about products and to persuade them to participate in an exchange.
Industry	A group of firms that produce identical or similar products is an industry. It is also used specifically to refer to an area of economic production focused on manufacturing which involves large amounts of capital investment before any profit can be realized, also called "heavy industry".
Marketing	Promoting and selling products or services to customers, or prospective customers, is referred to as marketing.
Expense	In accounting, an expense represents an event in which an asset is used up or a liability is incurred. In terms of the accounting equation, expenses reduce owners' equity.
Gain	In finance, gain is a profit or an increase in value of an investment such as a stock or bond. Gain is calculated by fair market value or the proceeds from the sale of the investment minus the sum of the purchase price and all costs associated with it.
Continental Airlines	Continental Airlines is an airline of the United States. Based in Houston, Texas, it is the 6th largest airline in the U.S. and the 8th largest in the world. Continental's tagline, since 1998, has been Work Hard, Fly Right.
Bid	A bid price is a price offered by a buyer when he/she buys a good. In the context of stock trading on a stock exchange, the bid price is the highest price a buyer of a stock is willing to pay for a share of that given stock.
Analyst	Analyst refers to a person or tool with a primary function of information analysis, generally with a more limited, practical and short term set of goals than a researcher.
Oligopoly	A market structure in which there are a small number of sellers, at least some of whose individual decisions about price or quantity matter to the others is an oligopoly.
Excess capacity	Excess capacity refers to plant resources that are underused when imperfectly competitive firms produce less output than that associated with purely competitive firms, who by definiation, are achieving minimum average total cost.

Property	Assets defined in the broadest legal sense. Property includes the unrealized receivables of a cash basis taxpayer, but not services rendered.
Profit	Profit refers to the return to the resource entrepreneurial ability; total revenue minus total cost.
Firm	An organization that employs resources to produce a good or service for profit and owns and operates one or more plants is referred to as a firm.
Preference	The act of a debtor in paying or securing one or more of his creditors in a manner more favorable to them than to other creditors or to the exclusion of such other creditors is a preference. In the absence of statute, a preference is perfectly good, but to be legal it must be bona fide, and not a mere subterfuge of the debtor to secure a future benefit to himself or to prevent the application of his property to his debts.
Consideration	Consideration in contract law, a basic requirement for an enforceable agreement under traditional contract principles, defined in this text as legal value, bargained for and given in exchange for an act or promise. In corporation law, cash or property contributed to a corporation in exchange for shares, or a promise to contribute such cash or property.
Contract	A contract is a "promise" or an "agreement" that is enforced or recognized by the law. In the civil law, a contract is considered to be part of the general law of obligations.
Legal system	Legal system refers to system of rules that regulate behavior and the processes by which the laws of a country are enforced and through which redress of grievances is obtained.
Interest	In finance and economics, interest is the price paid by a borrower for the use of a lender's money. In other words, interest is the amount of paid to "rent" money for a period of time.
Peak	Peak refers to the point in the business cycle when an economic expansion reaches its highest point before turning down. Contrasts with trough.
Nash equilibrium	The Nash equilibrium is a kind of solution concept of a game involving two or more players, where no player has anything to gain by changing only his or her own strategy unilaterally.
Game theory	The modeling of strategic interactions among agents, used in economic models where the numbers of interacting agents is small enough that each has a perceptible influence on the others is called game theory.
Devise	In a will, a gift of real property is called a devise.
Utility	Utility refers to the want-satisfying power of a good or service; the satisfaction or pleasure a consumer obtains from the consumption of a good or service.
Deed	A deed is a legal instrument used to grant a right. The deed is best known as the method of transferring title to real estate from one person to another.
Mistake	In contract law a mistake is incorrect understanding by one or more parties to a contract and may be used as grounds to invalidate the agreement. Common law has identified three different types of mistake in contract: unilateral mistake, mutual mistake, and common mistake.
Big Business	Big business is usually used as a pejorative reference to the significant economic and political power which large and powerful corporations (especially multinational corporations), are capable of wielding.
Union	A worker association that bargains with employers over wages and working conditions is called a union.
Incentive	An incentive is any factor (financial or non-financial) that provides a motive for a particular course of action, or counts as a reason for preferring one choice to the alternatives.

Exchange	The trade of things of value between buyer and seller so that each is better off after the trade is called the exchange.
Trough	Trough refers to the point in the business cycle when an economic contraction reaches its lowest point before turning up.
Social Security	Social security primarily refers to a field of social welfare concerned with social protection, or protection against socially recognized conditions, including poverty, old age, disability, unemployment, families with children and others.
Security	Security refers to a claim on the borrower future income that is sold by the borrower to the lender. A security is a type of transferable interest representing financial value.
Service	Service refers to a "non tangible product" that is not embodied in a physical good and that typically effects some change in another product, person, or institution. Contrasts with good.
Developed country	A developed country is one that enjoys a relatively high standard of living derived through an industrialized, diversified economy. Countries with a very high Human Development Index are generally considered developed countries.
Expense	In accounting, an expense represents an event in which an asset is used up or a liability is incurred. In terms of the accounting equation, expenses reduce owners' equity.
Arbitration	Arbitration is a form of mediation or conciliation, where the mediating party is given power by the disputant parties to settle the dispute by making a finding. In practice arbitration is generally used as a substitute for judicial systems, particularly when the judicial processes are viewed as too slow, expensive or biased. Arbitration is also used by communities which lack formal law, as a substitute for formal law.
Subgame perfect equilibrium	Subgame perfect equilibrium is an equilibrium such that players' strategies constitute a Nash equilibrium in every subgame of the original game. It may be found by backward induction, an iterative process for solving finite extensive form or sequential games.
Present value	The value today of a stream of payments and/or receipts over time in the future and/or the past, converted to the present using an interest rate. If X_t is the amount in period t and r the interest rate, then present value at time t=0 is $V = ?T /t$.
Economics	The social science dealing with the use of scarce resources to obtain the maximum satisfaction of society's virtually unlimited economic wants is an economics.
Frequency	Frequency refers to the speed of the up and down movements of a fluctuating economic variable; that is, the number of times per unit of time that the variable completes a cycle of up and down movement.
Retaliation	The use of an increased trade barrier in response to another country increasing its trade barrier, either as a way of undoing the adverse effects of the latter's action or of punishing it is retaliation.
Receiver	A person that is appointed as a custodian of other people's property by a court of law or a creditor of the owner, pending a lawsuit or reorganization is called a receiver.
Bid	A bid price is a price offered by a buyer when he/she buys a good. In the context of stock trading on a stock exchange, the bid price is the highest price a buyer of a stock is willing to pay for a share of that given stock.

101

Complement	A good that is used in conjunction with another good is a complement. For example, cameras and film would complement eachother.
Market	A market is, as defined in economics, a social arrangement that allows buyers and sellers to discover information and carry out a voluntary exchange of goods or services.
Supply	Supply is the aggregate amount of any material good that can be called into being at a certain price point; it comprises one half of the equation of supply and demand. In classical economic theory, a curve representing supply is one of the factors that produce price.
Imperfect competition	Any departure from perfect competition. However, imperfect competition usually refers to one of the market structures other than perfect competition.
General equilibrium	Equality of supply and demand in all markets of an economy simultaneously. The number of markets does not have to be large. The simplest Ricardian model has markets only for two goods and one factor, labor, but this is a general equilibrium model.
Exchange market	Exchange market refers to the market on which national currencies are bought and sold.
Production	The creation of finished goods and services using the factors of production: land, labor, capital, entrepreneurship, and knowledge.
Exchange	The trade of things of value between buyer and seller so that each is better off after the trade is called the exchange.
Edgeworth box	Edgeworth box refers to a graphic device used to demonstrate economic efficiency. Most frequently used to illustrate the contract curve in an exchange economy but also useful in the theory of production.
Preference	The act of a debtor in paying or securing one or more of his creditors in a manner more favorable to them than to other creditors or to the exclusion of such other creditors is a preference. In the absence of statute, a preference is perfectly good, but to be legal it must be bona fide, and not a mere subterfuge of the debtor to secure a future benefit to himself or to prevent the application of his property to his debts.
Endowment	Endowment refers to the amount of something that a person or country simply has, rather than their having somehow to acquire it.
Indifference curve	Indifference curve refers to a means of representing the preferences and well being of consumers. Formally, it is a curve representing the combinations of arguments in a utility function that yield a given level of utility.
Interest	In finance and economics, interest is the price paid by a borrower for the use of a lender's money. In other words, interest is the amount of paid to "rent" money for a period of time.
Consumption	In Keynesian economics consumption refers to personal consumption expenditure, i.e., the purchase of currently produced goods and services out of income, out of savings (net worth), or from borrowed funds. It refers to that part of disposable income that does not go to saving.
Economy	The income, expenditures, and resources that affect the cost of running a business and household are called an economy.
Holding	The holding is a court's determination of a matter of law based on the issue presented in the particular case. In other words: under this law, with these facts, this result.
Points	Loan origination fees that may be deductible as interest by a buyer of property. A seller of property who pays points reduces the selling price by the amount of the points paid for the buyer.
Pareto	Pareto efficient allocation refers to an allocation of resources in which no one individual

efficient allocation	can be made better off without making someone else worse off.
Efficient allocation	An allocation that it is impossible unambiguously to improve upon, in the sense of producing more of one good without producing less of another is an efficient allocation.
Pareto efficiency	A condition in which no change is possible that will make some members of society better off without making some other members of society worse off is referred to as pareto efficiency. It is a central concept in economics with broad applications in game theory, engineering and the social sciences.
Economics	The social science dealing with the use of scarce resources to obtain the maximum satisfaction of society's virtually unlimited economic wants is an economics.
Contract curve	Given some endowment in an Edgeworth box, the contract curve is the individually rational subset of the Pareto set. In other words, it is the set of Pareto efficient points such that both agents are at least as well off as under their endowment.
Contract	A contract is a "promise" or an "agreement" that is enforced or recognized by the law. In the civil law, a contract is considered to be part of the general law of obligations.
Gains from trade	The net increase in output that countries experience as a result of lowering import tariffs and otherwise liberalizing trade is referred to as gains from trade.
Gain	In finance, gain is a profit or an increase in value of an investment such as a stock or bond. Gain is calculated by fair market value or the proceeds from the sale of the investment minus the sum of the purchase price and all costs associated with it.
Competitive market	A market in which no buyer or seller has market power is called a competitive market.
Agent	A person who makes economic decisions for another economic actor. A hired manager operates as an agent for a firm's owner.
Total demand	Total demand refers to the demand schedule or the demand curve of all buyers of a good or service; also called market demand.
Excess demand	Demand minus supply. Thus a country's demand for imports of a homogeneous good is its excess demand for that good.
Context	The effect of the background under which a message often takes on more and richer meaning is a context. Context is especially important in cross-cultural interactions because some cultures are said to be high context or low context.
Excess supply	Supply minus demand. Thus a country's supply of exports of a homogeneous good is its excess supply of that good.
Competitive equilibrium	The balancing of supply and demand in a market or economy characterized by perfect competition is competitive equilibrium.
Budget line	Given an allocation of two goods, the budget line through that allocation is the set of all other allocations of the two goods that someone in a market could arrive at by selling one of the goods for the other.
Property	Assets defined in the broadest legal sense. Property includes the unrealized receivables of a cash basis taxpayer, but not services rendered.
Budget	Budget refers to an account, usually for a year, of the planned expenditures and the expected receipts of an entity. For a government, the receipts are tax revenues.
Total supply	Total supply refers to the supply schedule or the supply curve of all sellers of a good or service.

Budget set	A budget set includes all possible consumption bundles that someone can afford given the prices of goods and the person's income level. The budget set is bounded above by the budget line.
Budget constraint	Budget constraint refers to the maximum quantity of goods that could be purchased for a given level of income and a given set of prices.
Relative price	Relative price refers to the price of one thing in terms of another; i.e., the ratio of two prices.
Market price	Market price is an economic concept with commonplace familiarity; it is the price that a good or service is offered at, or will fetch, in the marketplace; it is of interest mainly in the study of microeconomics.
Numeraire	The unit in which prices are measured. This may be a currency, but in real models, such as most trade models, the numeraire is usually one of the goods, whose price is then set at one.
Equilibrium price	Equilibrium price refers to the price in a competitive market at which the quantity demanded and the quantity supplied are equal, there is neither a shortage nor a surplus, and there is no tendency for price to rise or fall.
Argument	The discussion by counsel for the respective parties of their contentions on the law and the facts of the case being tried in order to aid the jury in arriving at a correct and just conclusion is called argument.
Continuity	A media scheduling strategy where a continuous pattern of advertising is used over the time span of the advertising campaign is continuity.
Aggregate demand	The total demand for a country's output, including demands for consumption, investment, government purchases, and net exports is referred to as aggregate demand.
Aggregate demand function	The relationship between aggregate output and aggregate demand that shows the quantity of aggregate output demanded at each level of aggregate output is called aggregate demand function.
Purchasing	Purchasing refers to the function in a firm that searches for quality material resources, finds the best suppliers, and negotiates the best price for goods and services.
Welfare economics	Welfare economics refers to the branch of economic thought that deals with economic welfare, especially various propositions relating competitive general equilibrium to the efficiency and desirability of an allocation.
Welfare	Welfare refers to the economic well being of an individual, group, or economy. For individuals, it is conceptualized by a utility function. For groups, including countries and the world, it is a tricky philosophical concept, since individuals fare differently.
Offer curve	Offer curve refers to a curve showing, for a two-good model, the quantity of one good that a country will export for each quantity of the other that it imports.
Monopoly	A monopoly is defined as a persistent market situation where there is only one provider of a kind of product or service.
Utility	Utility refers to the want-satisfying power of a good or service; the satisfaction or pleasure a consumer obtains from the consumption of a good or service.
Resource allocation	Resource allocation refers to the manner in which an economy distributes its resources among the potential uses so as to produce a particular set of final goods.
First welfare theorem	In welfare economics, the first welfare theorem states that a competitive market economy will simultaneously lead to a Pareto efficient equilibrium and general competitive equilibrium. This was first demonstrated mathematically by economists Arrow and Debreu, although the

	restrictive assumptions necessary for the proof mean that the result may not necessarily reflect the workings of real economies.
Assignment	A transfer of property or some right or interest is referred to as assignment.
Slope	The slope of a line in the plane containing the x and y axes is generally represented by the letter m, and is defined as the change in the y coordinate divided by the corresponding change in the x coordinate, between two distinct points on the line.
Allocate	Allocate refers to the assignment of income for various tax purposes. A multistate corporation's nonbusiness income usually is distributed to the state where the nonbusiness assets are located; it is not apportioned with the rest of the entity's income.
Externality	Externality refers to an effect of one economic agent's actions on another, such that one agent's decisions make another better or worse off by changing their utility or cost.
Consumption externality	Any positive or negative third party effect arising from consumption is referred to as consumption externality.
Distribution	Distribution in economics, the manner in which total output and income is distributed among individuals or factors.
Market system	All the product and resource markets of a market economy and the relationships among them are called a market system.
Scarcity	Scarcity is defined as not having sufficient resources to produce enough to fulfill unlimited subjective wants. Alternatively, scarcity implies that not all of society's goals can be attained at the same time, so that trade-offs one good against others are made.
Policy	Similar to a script in that a policy can be a less than completely rational decision-making method. Involves the use of a pre-existing set of decision steps for any problem that presents itself.
Equity	Equity is the name given to the set of legal principles, in countries following the English common law tradition, which supplement strict rules of law where their application would operate harshly, so as to achieve what is sometimes referred to as "natural justice."
Consideration	Consideration in contract law, a basic requirement for an enforceable agreement under traditional contract principles, defined in this text as legal value, bargained for and given in exchange for an act or promise. In corporation law, cash or property contributed to a corporation in exchange for shares, or a promise to contribute such cash or property.
Tradeoff	The sacrifice of some or all of one economic goal, good, or service to achieve some other goal, good, or service is a tradeoff.
Purchasing power	The amount of goods that money will buy, usually measured by the CPI is referred to as purchasing power.
Fund	Independent accounting entity with a self-balancing set of accounts segregated for the purposes of carrying on specific activities is referred to as a fund.
Labor	People's physical and mental talents and efforts that are used to help produce goods and services are called labor.
Labor supply	The number of workers available to an economy. The principal determinants of labor supply are population, real wages, and social traditions.
Wage	The payment for the service of a unit of labor, per unit time. In trade theory, it is the only payment to labor, usually unskilled labor. In empirical work, wage data may exclude other compenzation, which must be added to get the total cost of employment.
Service	Service refers to a "non tangible product" that is not embodied in a physical good and that

Go to **Cram101.com** for the Practice Tests for this Chapter.

typically effects some change in another product, person, or institution. Contrasts with good.

Users
Users refer to people in the organization who actually use the product or service purchased by the buying center.

Market price	Market price is an economic concept with commonplace familiarity; it is the price that a good or service is offered at, or will fetch, in the marketplace; it is of interest mainly in the study of microeconomics.
Production	The creation of finished goods and services using the factors of production: land, labor, capital, entrepreneurship, and knowledge.
Market	A market is, as defined in economics, a social arrangement that allows buyers and sellers to discover information and carry out a voluntary exchange of goods or services.
Firm	An organization that employs resources to produce a good or service for profit and owns and operates one or more plants is referred to as a firm.
Economic model	Economic model refers to a simplified picture of economic reality; an abstract generalization.
Economy	The income, expenditures, and resources that affect the cost of running a business and household are called an economy.
Preference	The act of a debtor in paying or securing one or more of his creditors in a manner more favorable to them than to other creditors or to the exclusion of such other creditors is a preference. In the absence of statute, a preference is perfectly good, but to be legal it must be bona fide, and not a mere subterfuge of the debtor to secure a future benefit to himself or to prevent the application of his property to his debts.
Consumption	In Keynesian economics consumption refers to personal consumption expenditure, i.e., the purchase of currently produced goods and services out of income, out of savings (net worth), or from borrowed funds. It refers to that part of disposable income that does not go to saving.
Labor	People's physical and mental talents and efforts that are used to help produce goods and services are called labor.
Indifference curve	Indifference curve refers to a means of representing the preferences and well being of consumers. Formally, it is a curve representing the combinations of arguments in a utility function that yield a given level of utility.
Production function	Production function refers to a function that specifies the output in an industry for all combinations of inputs.
Argument	The discussion by counsel for the respective parties of their contentions on the law and the facts of the case being tried in order to aid the jury in arriving at a correct and just conclusion is called argument.
Slope	The slope of a line in the plane containing the x and y axes is generally represented by the letter m, and is defined as the change in the y coordinate divided by the corresponding change in the x coordinate, between two distinct points on the line.
Marginal product	In a production function, the marginal product of a factor is the increase in output due to a unit increase in the input of the factor; that is, the partial derivative of the production function with respect to the factor.
Marginal rate of substitution	In economics, the marginal rate of substitution is the rate at which consumers are willing to give up units of one good in exchange for more units of another good.
Labor market	Any arrangement that brings buyers and sellers of labor services together to agree on conditions of work and pay is called a labor market.
Profit	Profit refers to the return to the resource entrepreneurial ability; total revenue minus total cost.

Go to **Cram101.com** for the Practice Tests for this Chapter.

Go to **Cram101.com** for the Practice Tests for this Chapter.
And, **NEVER** highlight a book again!

Profit maximization	Search by a firm for the product quantity, quality, and price that gives that firm the highest possible profit is profit maximization.
Wage	The payment for the service of a unit of labor, per unit time. In trade theory, it is the only payment to labor, usually unskilled labor. In empirical work, wage data may exclude other compenzation, which must be added to get the total cost of employment.
Supply	Supply is the aggregate amount of any material good that can be called into being at a certain price point; it comprises one half of the equation of supply and demand. In classical economic theory, a curve representing supply is one of the factors that produce price.
Stock dividend	Stock dividend refers to pro rata distributions of stock or stock rights on common stock. They are usually issued in proportion to shares owned.
Shareholder	A shareholder is an individual or company (including a corporation) that legally owns one or more shares of stock in a joined stock company.
Dividend	Amount of corporate profits paid out for each share of stock is referred to as dividend.
Stock	In financial terminology, stock is the capital raized by a corporation, through the issuance and sale of shares.
Supply of labor	Supply of labor refers to the relationship between the quantity of labor supplied by employees and the real wage rate when all other influences on work plans remain the same.
Market system	All the product and resource markets of a market economy and the relationships among them are called a market system.
Budget line	Given an allocation of two goods, the budget line through that allocation is the set of all other allocations of the two goods that someone in a market could arrive at by selling one of the goods for the other.
Budget	Budget refers to an account, usually for a year, of the planned expenditures and the expected receipts of an entity. For a government, the receipts are tax revenues.
Marginal product of labor	Marginal product of labor refers to the increase in the amount of output from an additional unit of labor.
Market economy	A market economy is an economic system in which the production and distribution of goods and services takes place through the mechanism of free markets guided by a free price system rather than by the state in a planned economy.
Inputs	The inputs used by a firm or an economy are the labor, raw materials, electricity and other resources it uses to produce its outputs.
Technology	The body of knowledge and techniques that can be used to combine economic resources to produce goods and services is called technology.
Optimum	Optimum refers to the best. Usually refers to a most preferred choice by consumers subject to a budget constraint or a profit maximizing choice by firms or industry subject to a technological constraint.
Returns to scale	Returns to scale refers to a technical property of production that predicts what happens to output if the quantity of all input factors is increased by some amount of scale.
Decreasing returns to scale	Decreasing returns to scale refers to a property of a production function such that changing all inputs by the same proportion changes output less than in proportion. Example: a function homogeneous of degree less than one.
Constant returns to	Constant returns to scale refers to a property of a production function such that scaling all inputs by any positive constant also scales output by the same constant. Such a function is

scale	also called homogeneous of degree one or linearly homogeneous.
Competitive firm	Competitive firm refers to a firm without market power, with no ability to alter the market price of the goods it produces.
Budget set	A budget set includes all possible consumption bundles that someone can afford given the prices of goods and the person's income level. The budget set is bounded above by the budget line.
Increasing returns	An increase in a firm's output by a larger percentage than the percentage increase in its inputs is increasing returns.
Utility	Utility refers to the want-satisfying power of a good or service; the satisfaction or pleasure a consumer obtains from the consumption of a good or service.
Nonconvexity	Nonconvexity refers to the property of an economic model or system that sets representing technology, preferences, or constraints are not mathematically convex. Because convexity is needed for proof that competitive equilibrium is efficient and well-behaved, nonconvexities may imply market failures.
Competitive market	A market in which no buyer or seller has market power is called a competitive market.
Welfare	Welfare refers to the economic well being of an individual, group, or economy. For individuals, it is conceptualized by a utility function. For groups, including countries and the world, it is a tricky philosophical concept, since individuals fare differently.
First welfare theorem	In welfare economics, the first welfare theorem states that a competitive market economy will simultaneously lead to a Pareto efficient equilibrium and general competitive equilibrium. This was first demonstrated mathematically by economists Arrow and Debreu, although the restrictive assumptions necessary for the proof mean that the result may not necessarily reflect the workings of real economies.
Economic agents	Economic agents refers to individuals who engage in production, exchange, specialization, and consumption.
Points	Loan origination fees that may be deductible as interest by a buyer of property. A seller of property who pays points reduces the selling price by the amount of the points paid for the buyer.
Agent	A person who makes economic decisions for another economic actor. A hired manager operates as an agent for a firm's owner.
Efficient allocation of resources	Efficient allocation of resources refers to that allocation of an economy's resources among the production of different products that leads to the maximum satisfaction of consumers' wants.
Allocation of resources	Allocation of resources refers to the society's decisions on how to divide up its scarce input resources among the different outputs produced in the economy, and among the different firms or other organizations that produce those outputs.
Efficient allocation	An allocation that it is impossible unambiguously to improve upon, in the sense of producing more of one good without producing less of another is an efficient allocation.
Exchange	The trade of things of value between buyer and seller so that each is better off after the trade is called the exchange.
Competitive equilibrium	The balancing of supply and demand in a market or economy characterized by perfect competition is competitive equilibrium.
Externality	Externality refers to an effect of one economic agent's actions on another, such that one

Go to **Cram101.com** for the Practice Tests for this Chapter.

agent's decisions make another better or worse off by changing their utility or cost.

Pareto efficient allocation	Pareto efficient allocation refers to an allocation of resources in which no one individual can be made better off without making someone else worse off.
Production possibilities frontier	A graph that shows the combinations of output that the economy can possibly produce given the available factors of production and the available production technology is referred to as a production possibilities frontier; production possibilities curve.
Marginal rate of transformation	Marginal rate of transformation refers to the increase in output of one good made possible by a one-unit decrease in the output of another, given the technology and factor endowments of a country.
Tradeoff	The sacrifice of some or all of one economic goal, good, or service to achieve some other goal, good, or service is a tradeoff.
Comparative advantage	The ability to produce a good at lower cost, relative to other goods, compared to another country is a comparative advantage.
Pareto efficiency	A condition in which no change is possible that will make some members of society better off without making some other members of society worse off is referred to as pareto efficiency. It is a central concept in economics with broad applications in game theory, engineering and the social sciences.
Gains from trade	The net increase in output that countries experience as a result of lowering import tariffs and otherwise liberalizing trade is referred to as gains from trade.
Gain	In finance, gain is a profit or an increase in value of an investment such as a stock or bond. Gain is calculated by fair market value or the proceeds from the sale of the investment minus the sum of the purchase price and all costs associated with it.
Edgeworth box	Edgeworth box refers to a graphic device used to demonstrate economic efficiency. Most frequently used to illustrate the contract curve in an exchange economy but also useful in the theory of production.
Resource allocation	Resource allocation refers to the manner in which an economy distributes its resources among the potential uses so as to produce a particular set of final goods.
Variable	A variable is something measured by a number; it is used to analyze what happens to other things when the size of that number changes.
Endowment	Endowment refers to the amount of something that a person or country simply has, rather than their having somehow to acquire it.
Scarcity	Scarcity is defined as not having sufficient resources to produce enough to fulfill unlimited subjective wants. Alternatively, scarcity implies that not all of society's goals can be attained at the same time, so that trade-offs one good against others are made.
Policy	Similar to a script in that a policy can be a less than completely rational decision-making method. Involves the use of a pre-existing set of decision steps for any problem that presents itself.

Pareto efficiency	A condition in which no change is possible that will make some members of society better off without making some other members of society worse off is referred to as pareto efficiency. It is a central concept in economics with broad applications in game theory, engineering and the social sciences.
Distribution	Distribution in economics, the manner in which total output and income is distributed among individuals or factors.
Welfare	Welfare refers to the economic well being of an individual, group, or economy. For individuals, it is conceptualized by a utility function. For groups, including countries and the world, it is a tricky philosophical concept, since individuals fare differently.
Preference	The act of a debtor in paying or securing one or more of his creditors in a manner more favorable to them than to other creditors or to the exclusion of such other creditors is a preference. In the absence of statute, a preference is perfectly good, but to be legal it must be bona fide, and not a mere subterfuge of the debtor to secure a future benefit to himself or to prevent the application of his property to his debts.
Agent	A person who makes economic decisions for another economic actor. A hired manager operates as an agent for a firm's owner.
Yield	The interest rate that equates a future value or an annuity to a given present value is a yield.
Property	Assets defined in the broadest legal sense. Property includes the unrealized receivables of a cash basis taxpayer, but not services rendered.
Impossibility	A doctrine under which a party to a contract is relieved of his or her duty to perform when that performance has become impossible because of the occurrence of an event unforeseen at the time of contracting is referred to as impossibility.
Impossibility theorem	A proposition demonstrated by Kenneth Arrow showing that no system of aggregating individual preferences into social decisions will always yield consistent, non-arbitrary results is an impossibility theorem.
Social choice	Social choice refers to the problem of deciding what society wants in terms of public goods versus private goods.
Economics	The social science dealing with the use of scarce resources to obtain the maximum satisfaction of society's virtually unlimited economic wants is an economics.
Utility	Utility refers to the want-satisfying power of a good or service; the satisfaction or pleasure a consumer obtains from the consumption of a good or service.
Social welfare function	A social welfare function in welfare economics is a function that maps welfare measures for members of the society to a measure of aggregate welfare of the society.
Utility function	Utility function refers to a function that specifies the utility of a consumer for all combinations goods consumed. Represents both their welfare and their preferences.
Pareto efficient allocation	Pareto efficient allocation refers to an allocation of resources in which no one individual can be made better off without making someone else worse off.
Efficient allocation	An allocation that it is impossible unambiguously to improve upon, in the sense of producing more of one good without producing less of another is an efficient allocation.
Indifference curve	Indifference curve refers to a means of representing the preferences and well being of consumers. Formally, it is a curve representing the combinations of arguments in a utility function that yield a given level of utility.

Go to **Cram101.com** for the Practice Tests for this Chapter.
And, **NEVER** highlight a book again!

Paul Samuelson	Paul A. Samuelson (born May 15, 1915, in Gary, Indiana) is an American economist known for his work in many fields of economics. As professor of economics at the Massachusetts Institute of Technology, he has worked in fields including public finance theory, welfare economics, and monetary economics.
Contribution	In business organization law, the cash or property contributed to a business by its owners is referred to as contribution.
Competitive equilibrium	The balancing of supply and demand in a market or economy characterized by perfect competition is competitive equilibrium.
Lagrangian	A lagrangian refers to a function constructed in solving economic models that includes minimization and maximization of a function subject to constraints.
Variable	A variable is something measured by a number; it is used to analyze what happens to other things when the size of that number changes.

Externality	Externality refers to an effect of one economic agent's actions on another, such that one agent's decisions make another better or worse off by changing their utility or cost.
Production	The creation of finished goods and services using the factors of production: land, labor, capital, entrepreneurship, and knowledge.
Firm	An organization that employs resources to produce a good or service for profit and owns and operates one or more plants is referred to as a firm.
Market	A market is, as defined in economics, a social arrangement that allows buyers and sellers to discover information and carry out a voluntary exchange of goods or services.
Consumption	In Keynesian economics consumption refers to personal consumption expenditure, i.e., the purchase of currently produced goods and services out of income, out of savings (net worth), or from borrowed funds. It refers to that part of disposable income that does not go to saving.
Agent	A person who makes economic decisions for another economic actor. A hired manager operates as an agent for a firm's owner.
Economic agents	Economic agents refers to individuals who engage in production, exchange, specialization, and consumption.
Market price	Market price is an economic concept with commonplace familiarity; it is the price that a good or service is offered at, or will fetch, in the marketplace; it is of interest mainly in the study of microeconomics.
Consideration	Consideration in contract law, a basic requirement for an enforceable agreement under traditional contract principles, defined in this text as legal value, bargained for and given in exchange for an act or promise. In corporation law, cash or property contributed to a corporation in exchange for shares, or a promise to contribute such cash or property.
Preference	The act of a debtor in paying or securing one or more of his creditors in a manner more favorable to them than to other creditors or to the exclusion of such other creditors is a preference. In the absence of statute, a preference is perfectly good, but to be legal it must be bona fide, and not a mere subterfuge of the debtor to secure a future benefit to himself or to prevent the application of his property to his debts.
Edgeworth box	Edgeworth box refers to a graphic device used to demonstrate economic efficiency. Most frequently used to illustrate the contract curve in an exchange economy but also useful in the theory of production.
Consumption possibilities	The alternative combinations of goods and services that a country could consume in a given time period are consumption possibilities.
Endowment	Endowment refers to the amount of something that a person or country simply has, rather than their having somehow to acquire it.
Legal system	Legal system refers to system of rules that regulate behavior and the processes by which the laws of a country are enforced and through which redress of grievances is obtained.
Property	Assets defined in the broadest legal sense. Property includes the unrealized receivables of a cash basis taxpayer, but not services rendered.
Pareto efficient allocation	Pareto efficient allocation refers to an allocation of resources in which no one individual can be made better off without making someone else worse off.
Efficient allocation	An allocation that it is impossible unambiguously to improve upon, in the sense of producing more of one good without producing less of another is an efficient allocation.

Go to **Cram101.com** for the Practice Tests for this Chapter.

Points	Loan origination fees that may be deductible as interest by a buyer of property. A seller of property who pays points reduces the selling price by the amount of the points paid for the buyer.
Contract curve	Given some endowment in an Edgeworth box, the contract curve is the individually rational subset of the Pareto set. In other words, it is the set of Pareto efficient points such that both agents are at least as well off as under their endowment.
Contract	A contract is a "promise" or an "agreement" that is enforced or recognized by the law. In the civil law, a contract is considered to be part of the general law of obligations.
Property rights	Bundle of legal rights over the use to which a resource is put and over the use made of any income that may be derived from that resource are referred to as property rights.
Competitive equilibrium	The balancing of supply and demand in a market or economy characterized by perfect competition is competitive equilibrium.
Negotiation	Negotiation is the process whereby interested parties resolve disputes, agree upon courses of action, bargain for individual or collective advantage, and/or attempt to craft outcomes which serve their mutual interests.
Coase theorem	Coase theorem refers to the proposition that the allocation of property rights does not matter for economic efficiency, so long as they are well defined and a free market exists for the exchange of rights between those who have them and those who do not.
Assignment	A transfer of property or some right or interest is referred to as assignment.
Indifference curve	Indifference curve refers to a means of representing the preferences and well being of consumers. Formally, it is a curve representing the combinations of arguments in a utility function that yield a given level of utility.
Distribution	Distribution in economics, the manner in which total output and income is distributed among individuals or factors.
Distribution of property	Distribution of property is the division of property acquired during the course of a marriage. Nonexempt property of the bankruptcy estate must be distributed to the debtor's secured and an unsecured creditor pursuant to the statutory priority established by the Bankruptcy Code is called distribution of property.
Cost function	The relationship, expressed as an equation, between a cost and a one or more variables is the cost function. In choosing a cost function both economic plausibility and goodness fit are relevant. It measures how good any particular solution is.
Profit	Profit refers to the return to the resource entrepreneurial ability; total revenue minus total cost.
Social cost	Social cost, in economics, is the total of all the costs associated with an economic activity. It includes both costs borne by the economic agent and also all costs borne by society at large. It includes the costs reflected in the organization's production function and the costs external to the firm's private costs.
Economics	The social science dealing with the use of scarce resources to obtain the maximum satisfaction of society's virtually unlimited economic wants is an economics.
Journal	Book of original entry, in which transactions are recorded in a general ledger system, is referred to as a journal.
Profit maximization	Search by a firm for the product quantity, quality, and price that gives that firm the highest possible profit is profit maximization.
Merger	Merger refers to the combination of two firms into a single firm.

Yield	The interest rate that equates a future value or an annuity to a given present value is a yield.
Marginal cost	Marginal cost refers to the increase in cost that accompanies a unit increase in output; the partial derivative of the cost function with respect to output.
Private cost	Private cost refers to the cost to an individual economic agent, such as a consumer or firm, from an event, action, or policy change. Contrasts with social cost.
Marginal social cost	Marginal social cost equals the additional cost of producing one more unit of output.
Voucher	A voucher is an internally generated document that includes spaces for recording transaction data and designated authorizations.
Total cost	The sum of fixed cost and variable cost is referred to as total cost.
Quota	A government-imposed restriction on quantity, or sometimes on total value, used to restrict the import of something to a specific quantity is called a quota.
Control system	A control system is a device or set of devices that manage the behavior of other devices. Some devices or systems are not controllable. A control system is an interconnection of components connected or related in such a manner as to command, direct, or regulate itself or another system.
Credit	Credit refers to a recording as positive in the balance of payments, any transaction that gives rise to a payment into the country, such as an export, the sale of an asset, or borrowing from abroad.
Pareto efficiency	A condition in which no change is possible that will make some members of society better off without making some other members of society worse off is referred to as pareto efficiency. It is a central concept in economics with broad applications in game theory, engineering and the social sciences.
Welfare	Welfare refers to the economic well being of an individual, group, or economy. For individuals, it is conceptualized by a utility function. For groups, including countries and the world, it is a tricky philosophical concept, since individuals fare differently.
Supply	Supply is the aggregate amount of any material good that can be called into being at a certain price point; it comprises one half of the equation of supply and demand. In classical economic theory, a curve representing supply is one of the factors that produce price.
Present value	The value today of a stream of payments and/or receipts over time in the future and/or the past, converted to the present using an interest rate. If X_t is the amount in period t and r the interest rate, then present value at time t=0 is $V = ?T_l /t$.
Excess profit	Profit of a firm over and above what provides its owners with a normal return to capital is called excess profit.
Buyer	A buyer refers to a role in the buying center with formal authority and responsibility to select the supplier and negotiate the terms of the contract.
Internalize	Internalize refers to causing, usually by a tax or subsidy, an external cost or benefit of someone's actions to be experienced by them directly, so that they will take it into account in their decisions.
Tragedy of the commons	A parable that illustrates why common resources get used more than is desirable from the standpoint of society as a whole is known as tragedy of the commons.
Marginal product	In a production function, the marginal product of a factor is the increase in output due to a unit increase in the input of the factor; that is, the partial derivative of the production

function with respect to the factor.

Revenue	Revenue is a U.S. business term for the amount of money that a company receives from its activities, mostly from sales of products and/or services to customers.
Average product	The average product of a factor (i.e. labor, capital, etc.) in a firm or industry is its output divided by the amount of the factor employed. The total quantity of output divided the total quantity of some input.
Stock	In financial terminology, stock is the capital raized by a corporation, through the issuance and sale of shares.
Management	Management characterizes the process of leading and directing all or part of an organization, often a business, through the deployment and manipulation of resources. Early twentieth-century management writer Mary Parker Follett defined management as "the art of getting things done through people."
Industry	A group of firms that produce identical or similar products is an industry. It is also used specifically to refer to an area of economic production focused on manufacturing which involves large amounts of capital investment before any profit can be realized, also called "heavy industry".
Free market	A free market is a market where price is determined by the unregulated interchange of supply and demand rather than set by artificial means.
Controlling	A management function that involves determining whether or not an organization is progressing toward its goals and objectives, and taking corrective action if it is not is called controlling.
Incentive	An incentive is any factor (financial or non-financial) that provides a motive for a particular course of action, or counts as a reason for preferring one choice to the alternatives.
Operation	A standardized method or technique that is performed repetitively, often on different materials resulting in different finished goods is called an operation.
Levy	Levy refers to imposing and collecting a tax or tariff.
Policy	Similar to a script in that a policy can be a less than completely rational decision-making method. Involves the use of a pre-existing set of decision steps for any problem that presents itself.
Competitive market	A market in which no buyer or seller has market power is called a competitive market.
Consumption externality	Any positive or negative third party effect arising from consumption is referred to as consumption externality.

Go to **Cram101.com** for the Practice Tests for this Chapter.

Technology	The body of knowledge and techniques that can be used to combine economic resources to produce goods and services is called technology.
Industrial revolution	The Industrial Revolution is the stream of new technology and the resulting growth of output that began in England toward the end of the 18th century.
Economics	The social science dealing with the use of scarce resources to obtain the maximum satisfaction of society's virtually unlimited economic wants is an economics.
Property	Assets defined in the broadest legal sense. Property includes the unrealized receivables of a cash basis taxpayer, but not services rendered.
Economic analysis	The process of deriving economic principles from relevant economic facts are called economic analysis. It is the comparison, with money as the index, of those costs and benefits to the wider economy that can be reasonably quantified, including all social costs and benefits of a project.
Information technology	Information technology refers to technology that helps companies change business by allowing them to use new methods.
Production	The creation of finished goods and services using the factors of production: land, labor, capital, entrepreneurship, and knowledge.
Market	A market is, as defined in economics, a social arrangement that allows buyers and sellers to discover information and carry out a voluntary exchange of goods or services.
Browser	A program that allows a user to connect to the World Wide Web by simply typing in a URL is a browser.
Consumer theory	Consumer theory is a theory of economics. It relates preferences, indifference curves and budget constraints to consumer demand curves. The mathematical models that make up consumer theory can be used in a constrained optimization problem to estimate the optimal goods bundle for an individual buyer.
Complement	A good that is used in conjunction with another good is a complement. For example, cameras and film would complement eachother.
Competitor	Other organizations in the same industry or type of business that provide a good or service to the same set of customers is referred to as a competitor.
Competitive Strategy	An outline of how a business intends to compete with other firms in the same industry is called competitive strategy.
Motorola	The Six Sigma quality system was developed at Motorola even though it became most well known because of its use by General Electric. It was created by engineer Bill Smith, under the direction of Bob Galvin (son of founder Paul Galvin) when he was running the company.
Intel	Intel Corporation, founded in 1968 and based in Santa Clara, California, USA, is the world's largest semiconductor company. Intel is best known for its PC microprocessors, where it maintains roughly 80% market share.
Microsoft	Microsoft is a multinational computer technology corporation with 2004 global annual sales of US$39.79 billion and 71,553 employees in 102 countries and regions as of July 2006. It develops, manufactures, licenses, and supports a wide range of software products for computing devices.
Users	Users refer to people in the organization who actually use the product or service purchased by the buying center.
End user	End user refers to the ultimate user of a product or service.
Marginal cost	Marginal cost refers to the increase in cost that accompanies a unit increase in output; the

Go to **Cram101.com** for the Practice Tests for this Chapter.

partial derivative of the cost function with respect to output.

Fixed cost	The cost that a firm bears if it does not produce at all and that is independent of its output. The presence of a fixed cost tends to imply increasing returns to scale. Contrasts with variable cost.
Profit	Profit refers to the return to the resource entrepreneurial ability; total revenue minus total cost.
Marginal revenue	Marginal revenue refers to the change in total revenue obtained by selling one additional unit.
Revenue	Revenue is a U.S. business term for the amount of money that a company receives from its activities, mostly from sales of products and/or services to customers.
Firm	An organization that employs resources to produce a good or service for profit and owns and operates one or more plants is referred to as a firm.
Nash equilibrium	The Nash equilibrium is a kind of solution concept of a game involving two or more players, where no player has anything to gain by changing only his or her own strategy unilaterally.
Merger	Merger refers to the combination of two firms into a single firm.
Boeing	Boeing is the world's largest aircraft manufacturer by revenue. Headquartered in Chicago, Illinois, Boeing is the second-largest defense contractor in the world. In 2005, the company was the world's largest civil aircraft manufacturer in terms of value.
Industry	A group of firms that produce identical or similar products is an industry. It is also used specifically to refer to an area of economic production focused on manufacturing which involves large amounts of capital investment before any profit can be realized, also called "heavy industry".
Sony	Sony is a multinational corporation and one of the world's largest media conglomerates founded in Tokyo, Japan. One of its divisions Sony Electronics is one of the leading manufacturers of electronics, video, communications, and information technology products for the consumer and professional markets.
Licensing	Licensing is a form of strategic alliance which involves the sale of a right to use certain proprietary knowledge (so called intellectual property) in a defined way.
Patent	The legal right to the proceeds from and control over the use of an invented product or process, granted for a fixed period of time, usually 20 years. Patent is one form of intellectual property that is subject of the TRIPS agreement.
Configuration	An organization's shape, which reflects the division of labor and the means of coordinating the divided tasks is configuration.
Elasticity	In economics, elasticity is the ratio of the incremental percentage change in one variable with respect to an incremental percentage change in another variable. Elasticity is usually expressed as a positive number (i.e., an absolute value) when the sign is already clear from context.
Standardization	Standardization, in the context related to technologies and industries, is the process of establishing a technical standard among competing entities in a market, where this will bring benefits without hurting competition.
Switching costs	Switching costs is a term used in microeconomics, strategic management, and marketing to describe any impediment to a customer's changing of suppliers. In many markets, consumers are forced to incur costs when switching from one supplier to another. These costs are called switching costs and can come in many different shapes.

Go to **Cram101.com** for the Practice Tests for this Chapter.

Consumer surplus	The difference between the maximum that consumers would be willing to pay for a good and what they actually do pay is consumer surplus. For each unit of the good, this is the vertical distance between the demand curve and price.
Inelastic demand	Inelastic demand refers to product or resource demand for which the elasticity coefficient for price is less than 1. This means the resulting percentage change in quantity demanded is less than the percentage change in price. In other words, consumers are relatively less sensitive to changes in price.
Inelastic	Inelastic refers to having an elasticity less than one. For a price elasticity of demand, this means that expenditure falls as price falls. For an income elasticity, it means that expenditure share falls with income.
Monopoly power	Monopoly power is an example of market failure which occurs when one or more of the participants has the ability to influence the price or other outcomes in some general or specialized market.
Monopoly	A monopoly is defined as a persistent market situation where there is only one provider of a kind of product or service.
Service	Service refers to a "non tangible product" that is not embodied in a physical good and that typically effects some change in another product, person, or institution. Contrasts with good.
Present value	The value today of a stream of payments and/or receipts over time in the future and/or the past, converted to the present using an interest rate. If X t is the amount in period t and r the interest rate, then present value at time t=0 is V = ?T /t.
Interest rate	The rate of return on bonds, loans, or deposits. When one speaks of 'the' interest rate, it is usually in a model where there is only one.
Interest	In finance and economics, interest is the price paid by a borrower for the use of a lender's money. In other words, interest is the amount of paid to "rent" money for a period of time.
Discount	The difference between the face value of a bond and its selling price, when a bond is sold for less than its face value it's referred to as a discount.
Fixture	Fixture refers to a thing that was originally personal property and that has been actually or constructively affixed to the soil itself or to some structure legally a part of the land.
Equilibrium price	Equilibrium price refers to the price in a competitive market at which the quantity demanded and the quantity supplied are equal, there is neither a shortage nor a surplus, and there is no tendency for price to rise or fall.
Markup	Markup is a term used in marketing to indicate how much the price of a product is above the cost of producing and distributing the product.
America Online	In 2000 America Online and Time Warner announced plans to merge, and the deal was approved by the Federal Trade Commission on January 11, 2001. This merger was primarily a product of the Internet mania of the late-1990s, known as the Internet bubble. The deal is known as one of the worst corporate mergers in history, destroying over $200 billion in shareholder value.
Advertising	Advertising refers to paid, nonpersonal communication through various media by organizations and individuals who are in some way identified in the advertising message.
Externality	Externality refers to an effect of one economic agent's actions on another, such that one agent's decisions make another better or worse off by changing their utility or cost.
Consumption	In Keynesian economics consumption refers to personal consumption expenditure, i.e., the purchase of currently produced goods and services out of income, out of savings (net worth), or from borrowed funds. It refers to that part of disposable income that does not go to

	saving.
Utility	Utility refers to the want-satisfying power of a good or service; the satisfaction or pleasure a consumer obtains from the consumption of a good or service.
Complementary good	A complementary good refers to a product or service that is used together with another good. When the price of one falls, the demand for the other increases. Cameras and film are considered complementary goods.
Willingness to pay	Willingness to pay refers to the largest amount of money that an individual or group could pay, along with a change in policy, without being made worse off.
Purchasing	Purchasing refers to the function in a firm that searches for quality material resources, finds the best suppliers, and negotiates the best price for goods and services.
Supply	Supply is the aggregate amount of any material good that can be called into being at a certain price point; it comprises one half of the equation of supply and demand. In classical economic theory, a curve representing supply is one of the factors that produce price.
Contract	A contract is a "promise" or an "agreement" that is enforced or recognized by the law. In the civil law, a contract is considered to be part of the general law of obligations.
Demand curve	Demand curve refers to the graph of quantity demanded as a function of price, normally downward sloping, straight or curved, and drawn with quantity on the horizontal axis and price on the vertical axis.
Supply curve	Supply curve refers to the graph of quantity supplied as a function of price, normally upward sloping, straight or curved, and drawn with quantity on the horizontal axis and price on the vertical axis.
Business strategy	Business strategy, which refers to the aggregated operational strategies of single business firm or that of an SBU in a diversified corporation refers to the way in which a firm competes in its chosen arenas.
Promotion	Promotion refers to all the techniques sellers use to motivate people to buy products or services. An attempt by marketers to inform people about products and to persuade them to participate in an exchange.
Exchange	The trade of things of value between buyer and seller so that each is better off after the trade is called the exchange.
Network effects	Increases in the value of a product to each user, including existing users, as the total number of users rises are network effects.
Journal	Book of original entry, in which transactions are recorded in a general ledger system, is referred to as a journal.
Economic perspective	A viewpoint that envisions individuals and institutions making rational decisions by comparing the marginal benefits and marginal costs associated with their actions is an economic perspective.
Aid	Assistance provided by countries and by international institutions such as the World Bank to developing countries in the form of monetary grants, loans at low interest rates, in kind, or a combination of these is called aid. Aid can also refer to assistance of any type rendered to benefit some group or individual.
Management	Management characterizes the process of leading and directing all or part of an organization, often a business, through the deployment and manipulation of resources. Early twentieth-century management writer Mary Parker Follett defined management as "the art of getting things done through people."

Proprietary	Proprietary indicates that a party, or proprietor, exercises private ownership, control or use over an item of property, usually to the exclusion of other parties. Where a party, holds or claims proprietary interests in relation to certain types of property (eg. a creative literary work, or software), that property may also be the subject of intellectual property law (eg. copyright or patents).
Main product	Product from a joint production process that has a high sales value compared with the sales values of all other products of the joint production process is referred to as main product.
Corporation	A legal entity chartered by a state or the Federal government that is distinct and separate from the individuals who own it is a corporation. This separation gives the corporation unique powers which other legal entities lack.
Stock	In financial terminology, stock is the capital raized by a corporation, through the issuance and sale of shares.
Policy	Similar to a script in that a policy can be a less than completely rational decision-making method. Involves the use of a pre-existing set of decision steps for any problem that presents itself.
Foundation	A Foundation is a type of philanthropic organization set up by either individuals or institutions as a legal entity (either as a corporation or trust) with the purpose of distributing grants to support causes in line with the goals of the foundation.
Business model	A business model is the instrument by which a business intends to generate revenue and profits. It is a summary of how a company means to serve its employees and customers, and involves both strategy (what an business intends to do) as well as an implementation.
Intellectual property	In law, intellectual property is an umbrella term for various legal entitlements which attach to certain types of information, ideas, or other intangibles in their expressed form. The holder of this legal entitlement is generally entitled to exercise various exclusive rights in relation to its subject matter.
Shareware	Software that is copyrighted but distributed to potential customers free of charge is shareware.
Trial	An examination before a competent tribunal, according to the law of the land, of the facts or law put in issue in a cause, for the purpose of determining such issue is a trial. When the court hears and determines any issue of fact or law for the purpose of determining the rights of the parties, it may be considered a trial.
Yield	The interest rate that equates a future value or an annuity to a given present value is a yield.
Product differentiation	A strategy in which one firm's product is distinguished from competing products by means of its design, related services, quality, location, or other attributes is called product differentiation.
Holding	The holding is a court's determination of a matter of law based on the issue presented in the particular case. In other words: under this law, with these facts, this result.
Public relations	Public relations refers to the management function that evaluates public attitudes, changes policies and procedures in response to the public's requests, and executes a program of action and information to earn public understanding and acceptance.
Complementary products	Products that use similar technologies and can coexist in a family of products are called complementary products. They tend to be purchased jointly and whose demands therefore are related.
Negotiation	Negotiation is the process whereby interested parties resolve disputes, agree upon courses of

Go to **Cram101.com** for the Practice Tests for this Chapter.

	action, bargain for individual or collective advantage, and/or attempt to craft outcomes which serve their mutual interests.
Tradeoff	The sacrifice of some or all of one economic goal, good, or service to achieve some other goal, good, or service is a tradeoff.
Transactions cost	Any cost associated with bringing buyers and sellers together is referred to as transactions cost.

Property rights	Bundle of legal rights over the use to which a resource is put and over the use made of any income that may be derived from that resource are referred to as property rights.
Externality	Externality refers to an effect of one economic agent's actions on another, such that one agent's decisions make another better or worse off by changing their utility or cost.
Consumption	In Keynesian economics consumption refers to personal consumption expenditure, i.e., the purchase of currently produced goods and services out of income, out of savings (net worth), or from borrowed funds. It refers to that part of disposable income that does not go to saving.
Property	Assets defined in the broadest legal sense. Property includes the unrealized receivables of a cash basis taxpayer, but not services rendered.
Consumption externality	Any positive or negative third party effect arising from consumption is referred to as consumption externality.
Production	The creation of finished goods and services using the factors of production: land, labor, capital, entrepreneurship, and knowledge.
Profit	Profit refers to the return to the resource entrepreneurial ability; total revenue minus total cost.
Market	A market is, as defined in economics, a social arrangement that allows buyers and sellers to discover information and carry out a voluntary exchange of goods or services.
Economic agents	Economic agents refers to individuals who engage in production, exchange, specialization, and consumption.
Agent	A person who makes economic decisions for another economic actor. A hired manager operates as an agent for a firm's owner.
Public good	A good that is provided for users collectively where use by one does not preclude use of the same units of the good by others is referred to as public good. Police protection is an example of a public good.
Contribution	In business organization law, the cash or property contributed to a business by its owners is referred to as contribution.
Utility function	Utility function refers to a function that specifies the utility of a consumer for all combinations goods consumed. Represents both their welfare and their preferences.
Utility	Utility refers to the want-satisfying power of a good or service; the satisfaction or pleasure a consumer obtains from the consumption of a good or service.
Service	Service refers to a "non tangible product" that is not embodied in a physical good and that typically effects some change in another product, person, or institution. Contrasts with good.
Interest	In finance and economics, interest is the price paid by a borrower for the use of a lender's money. In other words, interest is the amount of paid to "rent" money for a period of time.
Budget constraint	Budget constraint refers to the maximum quantity of goods that could be purchased for a given level of income and a given set of prices.
Budget	Budget refers to an account, usually for a year, of the planned expenditures and the expected receipts of an entity. For a government, the receipts are tax revenues.
Willingness to pay	Willingness to pay refers to the largest amount of money that an individual or group could pay, along with a change in policy, without being made worse off.
Distribution	Distribution in economics, the manner in which total output and income is distributed among

219

individuals or factors.

Incentive	An incentive is any factor (financial or non-financial) that provides a motive for a particular course of action, or counts as a reason for preferring one choice to the alternatives.
Cost function	The relationship, expressed as an equation, between a cost and a one or more variables is the cost function. In choosing a cost function both economic plausibility and goodness fit are relevant. It measures how good any particular solution is.
Pareto efficient allocation	Pareto efficient allocation refers to an allocation of resources in which no one individual can be made better off without making someone else worse off.
Efficient allocation	An allocation that it is impossible unambiguously to improve upon, in the sense of producing more of one good without producing less of another is an efficient allocation.
Private good	A good or service that is subject to the exclusion principle and is provided by privately owned firms to consumers who are willing to pay for it is called private good.
Marginal rate of substitution	In economics, the marginal rate of substitution is the rate at which consumers are willing to give up units of one good in exchange for more units of another good.
Marginal cost	Marginal cost refers to the increase in cost that accompanies a unit increase in output; the partial derivative of the cost function with respect to output.
Margin	A deposit by a buyer in stocks with a seller or a stockbroker, as security to cover fluctuations in the market in reference to stocks that the buyer has purchased but for which he has not paid is a margin. Commodities are also traded on margin.
Preference	The act of a debtor in paying or securing one or more of his creditors in a manner more favorable to them than to other creditors or to the exclusion of such other creditors is a preference. In the absence of statute, a preference is perfectly good, but to be legal it must be bona fide, and not a mere subterfuge of the debtor to secure a future benefit to himself or to prevent the application of his property to his debts.
Indifference curve	Indifference curve refers to a means of representing the preferences and well being of consumers. Formally, it is a curve representing the combinations of arguments in a utility function that yield a given level of utility.
Social cost	Social cost, in economics, is the total of all the costs associated with an economic activity. It includes both costs borne by the economic agent and also all costs borne by society at large. It includes the costs reflected in the organization's production function and the costs external to the firm's private costs.
Firm	An organization that employs resources to produce a good or service for profit and owns and operates one or more plants is referred to as a firm.
Marginal benefit	Marginal benefit refers to the extra benefit of consuming 1 more unit of some good or service; the change in total benefit when 1 more unit is consumed.
Free rider	Free rider refers to someone who enjoys the benefits of a public good without bearing the cost. An example, in trade policy, is that trade liberalization benefits the majority of consumers without their lobbying for it.
Endowment	Endowment refers to the amount of something that a person or country simply has, rather than their having somehow to acquire it.
Slope	The slope of a line in the plane containing the x and y axes is generally represented by the letter m, and is defined as the change in the y coordinate divided by the corresponding change in the x coordinate, between two distinct points on the line.

Go to **Cram101.com** for the Practice Tests for this Chapter.

Competitive market	A market in which no buyer or seller has market power is called a competitive market.
Social choice	Social choice refers to the problem of deciding what society wants in terms of public goods versus private goods.
Valuation	In finance, valuation is the process of estimating the market value of a financial asset or liability. They can be done on assets (for example, investments in marketable securities such as stocks, options, business enterprises, or intangible assets such as patents and trademarks) or on liabilities (e.g., Bonds issued by a company).
Aid	Assistance provided by countries and by international institutions such as the World Bank to developing countries in the form of monetary grants, loans at low interest rates, in kind, or a combination of these is called aid. Aid can also refer to assistance of any type rendered to benefit some group or individual.
Auction	A preexisting business model that operates successfully on the Internet by announcing an item for sale and permitting multiple purchasers to bid on them under specified rules and condition is an auction.
Stated value	An arbitrary dollar amount assigned to shares by the board of directors, representing the minimum amount of consideration for which the corporation may issue the shares and the portion of consideration that must be allocated to the stated capital account is the stated value.
Devise	In a will, a gift of real property is called a devise.
Bid	A bid price is a price offered by a buyer when he/she buys a good. In the context of stock trading on a stock exchange, the bid price is the highest price a buyer of a stock is willing to pay for a share of that given stock.
Tradeoff	The sacrifice of some or all of one economic goal, good, or service to achieve some other goal, good, or service is a tradeoff.
Equity	Equity is the name given to the set of legal principles, in countries following the English common law tradition, which supplement strict rules of law where their application would operate harshly, so as to achieve what is sometimes referred to as "natural justice."
Political economy	Early name for the discipline of economics. A field within economics encompassing several alternatives to neoclassical economics, including Marxist economics. Also called radical political economy.
Journal	Book of original entry, in which transactions are recorded in a general ledger system, is referred to as a journal.
Economy	The income, expenditures, and resources that affect the cost of running a business and household are called an economy.
Variable	A variable is something measured by a number; it is used to analyze what happens to other things when the size of that number changes.
Supply	Supply is the aggregate amount of any material good that can be called into being at a certain price point; it comprises one half of the equation of supply and demand. In classical economic theory, a curve representing supply is one of the factors that produce price.

Market	A market is, as defined in economics, a social arrangement that allows buyers and sellers to discover information and carry out a voluntary exchange of goods or services.
Gain	In finance, gain is a profit or an increase in value of an investment such as a stock or bond. Gain is calculated by fair market value or the proceeds from the sale of the investment minus the sum of the purchase price and all costs associated with it.
Firm	An organization that employs resources to produce a good or service for profit and owns and operates one or more plants is referred to as a firm.
Labor market	Any arrangement that brings buyers and sellers of labor services together to agree on conditions of work and pay is called a labor market.
Labor	People's physical and mental talents and efforts that are used to help produce goods and services are called labor.
Asymmetric information	Asymmetric information refers to the failure of two parties to a transaction to have the same relevant information. Examples are buyers who know less about product quality than sellers, and lenders who know less about likely default than borrowers.
Buyer	A buyer refers to a role in the buying center with formal authority and responsibility to select the supplier and negotiate the terms of the contract.
Economics	The social science dealing with the use of scarce resources to obtain the maximum satisfaction of society's virtually unlimited economic wants is an economics.
Market failure	Any departure from the ideal benchmark of perfect competition, especially the complete absence of a market due to incomplete or asymmetric information is called market failure.
Externality	Externality refers to an effect of one economic agent's actions on another, such that one agent's decisions make another better or worse off by changing their utility or cost.
Willingness to pay	Willingness to pay refers to the largest amount of money that an individual or group could pay, along with a change in policy, without being made worse off.
Equilibrium price	Equilibrium price refers to the price in a competitive market at which the quantity demanded and the quantity supplied are equal, there is neither a shortage nor a surplus, and there is no tendency for price to rise or fall.
Pure competition	A market structure in which a very large number of firms sells a standardized product, into which entry is very easy, in which the individual seller has no control over the product price, and in which there is no non-price competition is pure competition.
Producer surplus	The difference between the revenue of producers and production cost, measured as the area above the supply curve and below price, out to the quantity supplied, and net of fixed cost and losses at low output is producer surplus. If input prices are constant, this is profit.
Marginal cost	Marginal cost refers to the increase in cost that accompanies a unit increase in output; the partial derivative of the cost function with respect to output.
Adverse selection	Adverse selection occurs under conditions of asymmetric information and refers to a self-selecting process where markets fail to price quality distinctions. One example is the tendency for insurance to be purchased only by those who are most likely to need it, thus raising its cost to healthy buyers as well as unhealthy buyers.
Supply	Supply is the aggregate amount of any material good that can be called into being at a certain price point; it comprises one half of the equation of supply and demand. In classical economic theory, a curve representing supply is one of the factors that produce price.
Market price	Market price is an economic concept with commonplace familiarity; it is the price that a good or service is offered at, or will fetch, in the marketplace; it is of interest mainly in the

Go to **Cram101.com** for the Practice Tests for this Chapter.

study of microeconomics.

Insurance	Insurance refers to a system by which individuals can reduce their exposure to risk of large losses by spreading the risks among a large number of persons.
Health insurance	Health insurance is a type of insurance whereby the insurer pays the medical costs of the insured if the insured becomes sick due to covered causes, or due to accidents. The insurer may be a private organization or a government agency.
Incidence	The ultimate economic effect of a tax on the real incomes of producers or consumers. Thus a sales tax may be paid by a retailer, but it is likely that the incidence falls upon the consumer.
Fringe benefits	The rewards other than wages that employees receive from their employers and that include pensions, medical and dental insurance, paid vacations, and sick leaves are referred to as fringe benefits.
Fringe benefit	Benefits such as sick-leave pay, vacation pay, pension plans, and health plans that represent additional compenzation to employees beyond base wages is a fringe benefit.
Moral hazard	Moral hazard arises when people behave recklessly because they know they will be saved if things go wrong.
Industry	A group of firms that produce identical or similar products is an industry. It is also used specifically to refer to an area of economic production focused on manufacturing which involves large amounts of capital investment before any profit can be realized, also called "heavy industry".
Incentive	An incentive is any factor (financial or non-financial) that provides a motive for a particular course of action, or counts as a reason for preferring one choice to the alternatives.
Users	Users refer to people in the organization who actually use the product or service purchased by the buying center.
Competitive market	A market in which no buyer or seller has market power is called a competitive market.
Rationing	Rationing is the controlled distribution of resources and scarce goods or services: it restricts how much people are allowed to buy or consume.
Intervention	Intervention refers to an activity in which a government buys or sells its currency in the foreign exchange market in order to affect its currency's exchange rate.
Warranty	An obligation of a company to replace defective goods or correct any deficiencies in performance or quality of a product is called a warranty.
Context	The effect of the background under which a message often takes on more and richer meaning is a context. Context is especially important in cross-cultural interactions because some cultures are said to be high context or low context.
Marginal product	In a production function, the marginal product of a factor is the increase in output due to a unit increase in the input of the factor; that is, the partial derivative of the production function with respect to the factor.
Wage	The payment for the service of a unit of labor, per unit time. In trade theory, it is the only payment to labor, usually unskilled labor. In empirical work, wage data may exclude other compenzation, which must be added to get the total cost of employment.
Productivity	Productivity refers to the total output of goods and services in a given period of time divided by work hours.

Interest	In finance and economics, interest is the price paid by a borrower for the use of a lender's money. In other words, interest is the amount of paid to "rent" money for a period of time.
Average product	The average product of a factor (i.e. labor, capital, etc.) in a firm or industry is its output divided by the amount of the factor employed. The total quantity of output divided the total quantity of some input.
Acquisition	A company's purchase of the property and obligations of another company is an acquisition.
Graduation	Termination of a country's eligibility for GSP tariff preferences on the grounds that it has progressed sufficiently, in terms of per capita income or another measure, that it is no longer in need to special and differential treatment is graduation.
Incentive system	An incentive system refers to plans in which employees can earn additional compenzation in return for certain types of performance.
Political economy	Early name for the discipline of economics. A field within economics encompassing several alternatives to neoclassical economics, including Marxist economics. Also called radical political economy.
Journal	Book of original entry, in which transactions are recorded in a general ledger system, is referred to as a journal.
Economy	The income, expenditures, and resources that affect the cost of running a business and household are called an economy.
Utility	Utility refers to the want-satisfying power of a good or service; the satisfaction or pleasure a consumer obtains from the consumption of a good or service.
Marginal benefit	Marginal benefit refers to the extra benefit of consuming 1 more unit of some good or service; the change in total benefit when 1 more unit is consumed.
Profit	Profit refers to the return to the resource entrepreneurial ability; total revenue minus total cost.
Total utility	The total amount of satisfaction derived from the consumption of a single product or a combination of products is total utility.
Residual claimant	The residual claimants (shareholders, partners, or sole proprieter) to a bankrupt organization receive any money that is left after all assets are sold and all creditors paid.
Residual	Residual payments can refer to an ongoing stream of payments in respect of the completion of past achievements.
Shareholder	A shareholder is an individual or company (including a corporation) that legally owns one or more shares of stock in a joined stock company.
Corporation	A legal entity chartered by a state or the Federal government that is distinct and separate from the individuals who own it is a corporation. This separation gives the corporation unique powers which other legal entities lack.
Bondholder	The individual or entity that purchases a bond, thus loaning money to the company that issued the bond is the bondholder.
Management	Management characterizes the process of leading and directing all or part of an organization, often a business, through the deployment and manipulation of resources. Early twentieth-century management writer Mary Parker Follett defined management as "the art of getting things done through people."
Stockholder	A stockholder is an individual or company (including a corporation) that legally owns one or more shares of stock in a joined stock company. The shareholders are the owners of a corporation. Companies listed at the stock market strive to enhance shareholder value.

Production	The creation of finished goods and services using the factors of production: land, labor, capital, entrepreneurship, and knowledge.
Household	An economic unit that provides the economy with resources and uses the income received to purchase goods and services that satisfy economic wants is called household.
Quota	A government-imposed restriction on quantity, or sometimes on total value, used to restrict the import of something to a specific quantity is called a quota.
Mistake	In contract law a mistake is incorrect understanding by one or more parties to a contract and may be used as grounds to invalidate the agreement. Common law has identified three different types of mistake in contract: unilateral mistake, mutual mistake, and common mistake.
Inputs	The inputs used by a firm or an economy are the labor, raw materials, electricity and other resources it uses to produce its outputs.
Technology	The body of knowledge and techniques that can be used to combine economic resources to produce goods and services is called technology.
Evaluation	The consumer's appraisal of the product or brand on important attributes is called evaluation.
Compromise	Compromise occurs when the interaction is moderately important to meeting goals and the goals are neither completely compatible nor completely incompatible.
Service	Service refers to a "non tangible product" that is not embodied in a physical good and that typically effects some change in another product, person, or institution. Contrasts with good.
Labor relations	The field of labor relations looks at the relationship between management and workers, particularly groups of workers represented by a labor union.
Communism	Communism refers to an economic system in which capital is owned by private government. Contrasts with capitalism.
Citibank	In April of 2006, Citibank struck a deal with 7-Eleven to put its ATMs in over 5,500 convenience stores in the U.S. In the same month, it also announced it would sell all of its Buffalo and Rochester New York branches and accounts to M&T Bank.
Comparative advantage	The ability to produce a good at lower cost, relative to other goods, compared to another country is a comparative advantage.
Interest rate	The rate of return on bonds, loans, or deposits. When one speaks of 'the' interest rate, it is usually in a model where there is only one.
Investment	Investment refers to spending for the production and accumulation of capital and additions to inventories. In a financial sense, buying an asset with the expectation of making a return.
Credit	Credit refers to a recording as positive in the balance of payments, any transaction that gives rise to a payment into the country, such as an export, the sale of an asset, or borrowing from abroad.
Entrepreneur	The owner/operator. The person who organizes, manages, and assumes the risks of a firm, taking a new idea or a new product and turning it into a successful business is an entrepreneur.
Lender	Suppliers and financial institutions that lend money to companies is referred to as a lender.
Adoption	In corporation law, a corporation's acceptance of a pre-incorporation contract by action of its board of directors, by which the corporation becomes liable on the contract, is referred to as adoption.

Go to **Cram101.com** for the Practice Tests for this Chapter.

Agent	A person who makes economic decisions for another economic actor. A hired manager operates as an agent for a firm's owner.
Shares	Shares refer to an equity security, representing a shareholder's ownership of a corporation. Shares are one of a finite number of equal portions in the capital of a company, entitling the owner to a proportion of distributed, non-reinvested profits known as dividends and to a portion of the value of the company in case of liquidation.

Go to **Cram101.com** for the Practice Tests for this Chapter.

Printed in the United States
68104LVS00006B/187-188

9 781428 810372